Anthony Pagden was educated in Santiago de Chile, London, Barcelona and Oxford. He has been a publisher in Paris and a translator in Rome. In the past eighteen years, he has been a Reader in Intellectual History at Cambridge, a Fellow of Kings College, Cambridge, Professor at the European University Institute, a Visiting Professor at Harvard and Professor of History at Johns Hopkins University. He is currently Professor of History and Political Science at the University of California, Los Angeles. He is a regular contributor to the *TLS*, *New Republic* and *New York Times*.

PEOPLES AND EMPIRES

EUROPEANS AND THE REST OF THE WORLD, FROM ANTIQUITY TO THE PRESENT

Anthony Pagden

PHOENIX
PRESS

5 UPPER SAINT MARTIN'S LANE
LONDON
WC2H 9EA

A PHOENIX PRESS PAPERBACK

First published in Great Britain in 2001
by Weidenfeld & Nicolson
This paperback edition published in 2002
by Phoenix Press,
an imprint of Orion Books Ltd,
Orion House, 5 Upper St Martin's Lane,
London WC2H 9EA

A CIP catalogue record for this book
is available from the British Library.

ISBN 1 84212 495 1

Printed and bound in Great Britain by
Clays Ltd, St Ives plc

Contents

For Giulia

Prologue

This is a very short book on a very big subject – so big indeed that it could simply be described as the history of the world. It is the story of the transformation of groups of peoples into the massive states we call empires. However we choose to define the term – and it is, at best, a vague one – there have been empires in Africa, in Asia, in the Americas and in Europe. I am, however, largely concerned with the story of those empires of what is now called the West, from the rise of Alexander the Great to the collapse of the Soviet Union. I discuss China and Vijayanagara, or Safavid Iran only in so far as they touch upon that story. This is not because I imagine, as some do, that the Chinese or the Indians or the Iranians ultimately lacked the inventiveness, imaginative drive, or individuality which, supposedly, allowed the Europeans to dominate so much of the world. It is simply that since those other places have had their own histories, which have gone in sometimes quite different directions, it would require other books fully to tell them.

As with all books of this kind, which try to cover so much ground and so much historical time, I have relied on the goodwill of colleagues and friends to provide me with information and advice. Bill Rowe and Mathew Roller patiently answered my questions about the Chinese and Roman worlds respectively. I have learned from Sanjay Subrahmanyam and Serge Grunzinski how to think globally, as much as about the individual histories of India, Iran and Spanish America. I owe a very special debt to the students of my class on empires and imperialism at the School for Advanced International Studies in Washington who provided me with information, questioned my more dubious assertions and, in their polyglot cosmopolitan enthusiasms, taught me much about the roots of restlessness. An earlier version of the text was read with great care by Toby Mundy at Weidenfeld & Nicolson and by Scott Moyers at Random House, and their careful, detailed comments have improved the final version immeasurably. I am grateful to them for their patience and perceptiveness. I am grateful, too, to Rebecca Wilson and Alice Hunt for their guidance in the final stages.

Giulia Sissa taught me about ancient Greece, and about life, and to her all of this is gratefully dedicated.

Paris, August 2000

Introduction

In 'The Story of the Warrior and the Captive', the Argentine writer Jorge Luis Borges tells two stories. In the first, a Lombard 'barbarian' named Droctulft reaches the gates of the Byzantine city of Ravenna, the last outpost of the crumbling empire of Constantine the Great. He has come there as a conqueror. Until that moment, which will change his life in ways over which he will have no further control, his only concern has been war and its spoils. His is a world of movement, of horses and tents, of transhumance and conflict. He knows nothing of cities, or of the arts or the sciences, or of the measurement of time. His world is his people. His loyalty, as Borges says, is to his chief, his tribe, 'not to the universe'. Space is infinite only because he knows nothing of its limits. He fights against men whose languages he does not understand and whose ways of life he cannot comprehend. He senses that these others, who live in cities, have goods that he desires and that his people cannot create for themselves.

On the day on which he enters the city he becomes another, a stranger to what he was. He becomes aware of desires he has never known before, is seized with wonder at the palaces and squares, the domes and cupolas, of the great city. This was what he had come to plunder. Overwhelmed by it all, he now realizes that he has no choice but to change allegiances and to fight in

I

order to preserve what he had once thought only to destroy. By doing so, he acquires what he never knew he wanted: a place. There he will always be an outsider, a 'barbarian'. Because of that he will be compelled, as Borges says, to be little more than a child or a dog. But he and his descendants will have begun the long journey on the road towards the condition that Europeans have for centuries called 'civilization'.

Droctulft made one kind of journey. Borges' second story is about another. As a young woman, Borges' English grandmother was brought by her husband to the Pampas, the seemingly endless Argentine grasslands, staring at which, Charles Darwin once said, gave him 'horizontal vertigo'. There she met an English-woman, from Yorkshire, who as a child had been carried off in an Indian raid, had been raised as an Indian, and had married a chieftain to whom she had borne two sons. Borges' grandmother, shocked by what she could glimpse 'behind her story', the 'feasts of scorched meat or raw entrails ... the polygamy, the stench and the superstition', urged her to leave, to return to the world as she had once known it. But 'The woman answered that she was happy, and returned that night to the desert.'

Droctulft and the Indian captive crossed in opposite directions. This book is about the implications of those two stories, and the points at which they meet, cross and sometimes become confused one with the other. It is about what drives peoples into contact – and conflict – with one another. It is about restlessness. It is also, inevitably, about cruelty and anger, indifference and power, about loss and the passing of time. It is about empires and the peoples who have created them, and been created by them.

Empires, however we define the term, and wherever they occur, have always been way of imposing stability upon different groups who often have little love for one another. Most empires have offered their subject peoples a combination of opportunities and restraints. Many have chosen to accept the opportunities and put up with the restraints. Others, inevitably, have not. All, however, knew that what an empire of the size and power of Rome represented was what Droctulft had seen, in its final fading glory, at Ravenna. It was accumulated wealth, the comforts that a highly stratified, technologically advanced society can bring – at least for those who can afford them. It was – and, in the accounts from which Borges took his tale, this is what seems most to have persuaded Droctulft to devote himself to its preservation – the sheer sumptuousness of creativity: the paintings, the buildings, the garments of the peoples. It was also, although by the eighth century of the Christian era this was already a thing of the past, the possibility of security at least from external threat, of a calm and reflective life.

By contrast, the things Borges' grandmother could see in the life of the young English captive conjured up only images of a life of constant movement, a life lived in the open, a life without shape or ultimate purpose. For her, as for all Europeans, the only life in which it was possible to be fully human, to be, as she would have said, 'civilized', was one lived in cities. Our entire political and social vocabulary derives from this fact. 'Politics' and 'polity' have their root in the Greek term *polis*. Similarly 'civil', 'civility', 'civilization' all have their origins in the Latin word *civitas*. In time both words became abstract nouns translatable as the 'state', or the 'commonwealth'. But both had originally described the self-contained, urban spaces of the ancient world. Rome was the 'Eternal City', the 'Prince of Cities', which, in the words of the fourth-century poet Claudian, was the 'mother of arms, who casts empire [*imperium*] over all'.[1] The founding of empires has, therefore, always been closely associated with the creation of cities. Alexander the Great – whom we shall meet again – founded literally dozens in his name: in Egypt (the greatest of them, and the only one still to be called 'Alexandria'); at Herat in central Iran; at Arachosia (probably modern Kandahar); at Begram in the Hindu Kush; at Eschate (modern Leninabad). In one single year, 328 BC, he created six new cities north of the river Oxus. According to the Roman philosopher and historian Plutarch (although he was surely exaggerating), during the course of his reign Alexander established no less than seventy new settlements. Centuries later, when the Spanish conquistador Hernán Cortés marched through Mexico in 1519–20 he, too, founded cities as he went, first on the coast at Veracruz, then Cholula and Tlaxcala. Finally, after the great Aztec capital of Tenochtitlán had fallen in 1522, he rebuilt it and renamed it Mexico City.

Cities were, of course, by no means unique to Europe. Like much else that is defining of European culture, the walled, largely self-governing urban space had originated in Asia. But it is only with the rise of Athens after the sixth century BC that an association in the European political imagination began to form between an urban environment and a particular way of life. Man, said the Greek philosopher Aristotle, was *zoon politikon* – a term which means, quite literally, an animal 'made for life in the polis'. In the Greek world life in the *polis* was not merely the best attainable existence. It was the only life in which it was possible for humanity to achieve the ends that nature, or the gods, had established for it. Little wonder then that for Aristotle there could be no life beyond the limits of the city but that of 'beasts and gods'. For centuries, those who chose, or were compelled, to leave their native cities were looked upon both as potentially degenerate and as potentially dangerous. Exile in the ancient world was a punishment comparable to death, and in Renaissance Europe it was often described, quite precisely, as a 'civil death'.

Those who have chosen to live beyond the limits of the city, the travellers and vagrants, even pilgrims, have in the course of European history been widely persecuted and abused. The most extreme case is that of Europe's Gypsies, whose history passes from initial astonishment and sympathy for what were believed to be the victims of the Ottoman conquest of the Byzantine empire, to suspicion and finally, in the gas chambers of Hitler's Reich, to attempted annihilation.

Yet, for all this distrust of journeying, this horror of the rootless and the homeless, most humans are, as St Francis once described them, *homines viatores*, perennial movers. When she met the young Englishwoman, Borges' grandmother was herself living on the frontier which, in nineteenth-century Argentina, was merely a step away from the condition of the Indians that so disgusted her. Most of us simply cannot avoid movement. Just as even the fiercest of endogamous societies must, on occasions, allow its members to 'marry out' if it is to survive, so all cultures, however concerned they might be with the virtues of immobility, have also to move if they are to progress. There have been few peoples for whom a state of permanent immobility is the norm. The happy Polynesians – the 'noble savages' – who figure so prominently in the eighteenth-century literary imagination of France, who went nowhere and who commanded all those Europeans who visited them to go home at once, could never, as the German philosopher Immanuel Kant said of them, 'give a satisfactory answer to the question of why they should exist at all'. Kant was being unduly harsh, not so much because the Tahitians had no desire to travel as because of his suspicion of what he took to be the description of a life of 'mere' enjoyment.[2] But he was right to see something inhuman in this idealization of Tahitian society.

Human history ends, as Kant insisted, as the history of settlement, of order, of peace and law. But it began in movement, in restlessness, in the quest for new resources, the search for more hospitable climates, and the insatiable desire for possession. These impulses drove the first humans out of Africa and across the world, and they continue to drive their descendants to this day. Probably all the cultures of all the races of the world have been the creations of prolonged periods of migration. Most of the stories we tell ourselves about our pasts, and many about our futures, are, therefore, stories of peregrination.

One such story, and it is typical of many early European accounts of the origins of humanity, is to be found in a curious collection of texts from the third century AD, known as the *Corpus Hermeticum*, supposedly the writings of the magus Hermes Trismegistus, whose wisdom was believed to predate even that of Moses. Here the Greek god Hermes is shown at work imprisoning the demiurges – the beings who had helped in the creation of the universe – in human bodies as a punishment for their attempt to rival the creativity of the gods. Even as he does so, the figure of Sarcasm (*Momos*) appears to congratulate him. 'It is a courageous thing you have done to have created man,' he mocks, 'this being with curious eyes and a bragging tongue ... For he will push his designing thoughts even to the limits of the earth. [These men] will extend their audacious busy hands even to the edge of the sea. They will cut down the forests, and will drive them [i.e. as ships] over the seas from bank to bank, all the way to those lands that are furthest away.'[3] As they travelled, these new and still more troublesome demiurges came together into families and then into tribes, all speaking separate languages and pursuing separate ways of life. This is the origin of peoples. Once divided, the stronger begin to seize possession of the weaker. This is the beginning of empire.

But what exactly is an empire? Macedonia, Rome, Byzantium, Ottoman Turkey, China, Peru, Mexico, the Soviet Union, the United States, even, by its enemies, the European Union, have all been described as 'empires'. We talk of 'informal' and 'economic' empires, of 'business' empires, even of the empire of the heart or reason's empire. 'Empire' has become as much a metaphor as the description of a particular kind of society. Today, the word is generally used as a term of abuse, although one that is also often tinged with nostalgia. 'Empire' suggests either the ruthless exploitation of largely defenceless, technologically unsophisticated peoples by the forces of technologically sophisticated ones – the kinds of empires carved out first in the Americas, then in Asia, and finally in Australia and the islands of the Pacific, by successive European powers. Or it conjures up images of the Third Reich or Stalinist Russia, where oppressor and oppressed come from much the same kind of cultures, and possess much the same kind of technologies. In both cases the 'empire' is represented as a mode of political oppression, a denial by one people of the rights – above all the right to self-determination – of countless others.

Empires, it is assumed, are in some sense artificial creations. They are created by conquest, and conquerors have always attempted to keep those they have conquered in subservience. This has been achieved by a mixture of simple force and some kind of ideology; in the case of the Roman empire this ideology was that of 'civilization', the lure of a more desirable, more comfortable and infinitely richer way of life. In the case of the Spanish, French and British empires, it was the same, but reinforced now by differing brands of Christianity. In the case of the Ottomans it was Islam, and in the case of the Soviet Union, Marxism. It is also assumed that virtually all of those who live under imperial rule would much rather not, and that sooner or later they will rise up and drive out their conquerors. Much of this, as we shall see, is undeniable, but by no means all of it. Empire has been a way of life for most of the peoples of the world, as either conqueror or conquered; and what we chose to call 'empires' have not only varied greatly from place to place and time to time, but have also marked the lives of those they involved in sometimes radically different ways.[4]

The modern term 'empire' and all its variants, 'emperor', 'imperialism', etc., derive, significantly, from the Latin word *imperium*, which in ancient Rome indicated supreme power involving both command in war and the magistrates' right to execute the law. The term has therefore linked the history of European imperialism very closely to the legacy of the Roman empire. Originally it meant little more than 'sovereignty', a sense which it retained until at least the eighteenth century. Ever since the days of the Roman republic, however, 'empire' has also been a word used to describe government over vast territories. When, for instance, in the early first century AD, the historian Tacitus spoke of the Roman world as an 'immense body of empire' he was alluding as much to its size as to its sovereignty, and ultimately it would be size which separated empires from mere kingdoms and principalities.[5] In 1914, the great Norwegian polar explorer Fridtjof Nansen calculated that the Russian empire had been expanding at an average daily rate of fifty-five square miles for over four centuries, or more than 20,000 square miles per year, an area roughly the size of modern Belgium. In terms of territory, the Russian empire was the largest the world has ever known, although most of it was unoccupied. But similar sorts of figures could be conjured up for most other imperial peoples. Under Philip II, the father of Alexander the Great, the Macedonian monarchy ceased at the Aegean and the Black Sea. By the time of Alexander's death in 323 BC, it reached from the Adriatic to the Indus, from the Punjab to the Sudan. In 1400, the empire of Timur – Christopher Marlowe's Tamburlaine – ran from the Black Sea to the gates of Kashgar. The Ottoman sultanate, which in the thirteenth century had been a small Anatolian province of *ghazi* ('holy') warriors sandwiched between the Byzantine empire and the Seljuk Turks, had by the beginning of the sixteenth century extended itself over more than 6,000 miles from Hungary to Central Asia. By the time the armies of Francisco Pizarro reached Peru in 1532, the domain of the Inca, which in the early fifteenth century had been limited to the region around Cuzco, stretched north through what are today Peru, Ecuador and

Colombia and south into Bolivia, northern Chile and north-west Argentina.

Because they have been large and relentlessly expansive, empires have also embraced peoples who have held a wide variety of different customs and beliefs, and often spoken an equally large number of different languages. It was in their sheer variety as much as their size that both their identity and their glory were to be found. The greatness of the Romans, said the second-century-BC Greek historian Polybius, lay in the fact that they now ruled over peoples of whom Alexander the Great had never even heard. Sixteen hundred years later, Spanish historians of the empire of Charles V would make much the same observation about their emperor.

Because of their size and sheer diversity, most empires have in time become cosmopolitan societies. In order to rule vast and widely separated domains, imperial governments have generally found themselves compelled to be broadly tolerant of diversity of culture and sometimes even of belief, so long as these posed no threat to their authority. In such extensive societies it was frequently a matter of indifference whether the supreme lord was a king in London or an emperor in Delhi. In many cases it might be preferable to be ruled by a distant sovereign than one close to hand. Better, said the Milanese in the sixteenth century, trapped between the contending powers of Spain and France, a king in Madrid than one in Paris. Madrid, at least, was further away.

But if they have generally tolerated diversity, empires have also inevitably transformed the peoples whom they have brought together. 'Empire,' said Charles Maurice de Talleyrand, Napoleon's foreign minister, in 1797, is 'the art of putting men in their place.' And putting men in their place inevitably resulted in prolonged and extensive migrations. Some of these were voluntary, the movement of the dispossessed, or, as happened in America and Asia, and later in Africa, of the marginalized in search of a better and richer life. Some, however, such as the Atlantic slave-trade – the greatest and most nefarious of them all – or the British transportation of indentured Indian servants in the 1840s to what Lord Salisbury called the 'warmer' British possessions, Mauritius, Trinidad, Fiji and Natal, were wholly involuntary.[6]

All the way from Europe to the Americas, these migrations have inevitably destroyed societies that were once flourishing. They have also brought into being entire societies that did not exist before. And in time these have created new peoples. The inhabitants of modern Greece and the Balkans are not what they were under Alexander, neither are the modern Italians Romans, nor the black populations of the Americas much like the West African peoples from whom they are descended. The majority of the inhabitants of Spanish America are neither fully European nor wholly Indian but, as the 'Liberator' Simón Bolívar said of them in 1810, 'a sort of middle species between the legitimate owners of this land and the Spanish usurpers'.

Empires have severely limited the freedoms of some peoples, but they have also given others opportunities they could not otherwise have imagined. As the 'father' of modern India, Jawaharlal Nehru, once observed, 'a foreign conquest, with all its evils, has one advantage: it widens the mental horizon of the people and compels them to look out of their shells. They realize that the world is much bigger and a more variegated place than they had imagined.'[7] In this way empires have been an inseparable part, real as well as metaphorical, of the development and spread of human knowledge. The 'through passage of the world', reflected Francis Bacon in 1620, by which he meant as much its occupation as its navigation, was clearly 'destined by divine providence' to be achieved in the same age as the 'advancement of learning'.[8]

Empires have, of course, also been responsible for a great deal of human suffering. They have been responsible, in the Americas and the Pacific, for the elimination of entire peoples, and have caused perhaps irreversible damage to vast areas of the surface of the planet. Now they are no more, at least in their traditional form. But they have, for centuries, comprised the history of the human race.

I *The first world conqueror*

The story of the empires of the peoples of Europe begins in ancient Greece. For the Greeks, who devised the vocabularies with which we still think about how to live our lives, were also, as they described themselves, 'extreme travellers'. The Cyclopes, one of whom devoured members of Odysseus' crew, were the embodiment of barbarism because, among their other defects, they knew nothing of navigation and had never left their island home. Travel, as we know, broadens the mind. The first person to have made the connection between voyaging (*planê*) and wisdom (*sophia*) was supposedly Solon, who also gave the Athenians their laws and thus created the first true political society in European history.¹ Subsequent Greek history is filled with wanderers in search of knowledge. Sometime in the fifth century BC, Herodotus, the 'father of history', travelled well beyond the limits of his world, to Egypt and Libya, Babylon and the Phoenician city of Tyre, even to southern Russia, and reported extensively on what he found there. Pythagoras, the great sixth-century-BC mathematician, journeyed from his native Samos to Egypt and Crete before settling finally in Croton in southern Italy; and the earliest of the ancient geographers, Hecateus of Miletus, visited Egypt even before Herodotus.

The knowledge to be gained from travel was almost always, however, also a means to possession. The Greeks were not only great travellers, they were also great colonizers. Beginning in the eighth century BC when Corinth established a colony on what is today Corfu, the Greek city-states moved steadily across the entire Mediterranean until by 580 BC they had occupied, to some degree, all the most obviously desirable areas in the world then available to them.[2] Colonization and conquest on this scale required, obviously, skilled navigators and relatively large ships. Most of all, however, it required the evolution of a certain kind of warfare. Immanuel Kant believed that human conflict was nature's means of forcing primitive men to leave the settled, comfortable boundaries of their homes. There, like grazing cattle, they might be happy, but because they were not also anxious and active they could not be properly human. Kant credited nature with too much insight. But, in one way or another, war has contributed more than any other single factor to the steady distribution of peoples around the world.

Yet if all peoples engage in some kind of warfare, wars themselves are of many different kinds. The conflicts which took place between the tribal peoples of North and South America, parts of East Africa and Australia, and which still occur among the few remaining peoples of the world's rainforests, are often harsh, cruel and sudden; but they rarely do, or are intended to do, much lasting damage. Such struggles are, as one sympathetic Spanish observer in the sixteenth century described them, 'no more deadly than our jousting, or than many European children's games'.[3] They are fought for limited and often symbolic gains, and rarely aim at conquest or subjugation. They are not intended to change the world.

The kind of war of which Kant was thinking was something very different. It emerged out of the eastern Mediterranean and the Steppes in the late Bronze Age. It is the warfare celebrated in the *Iliad*, and it aimed at the total transformation of entire peoples or sometimes, as in the Trojan War, at their ultimate destruction. The Trojan War, not only the best-known but also one of the longest recorded wars in history, ushered in a new era in human conflict, at least in the Mediterranean. Agamemnon and his crew of semi-divine warriors had no objective beyond revenge for the insult inflicted upon the Spartan Menelaus by a Trojan prince. They were not conquerors, much less empire-builders. When they finally left after ten long years of unceasing conflict, Troy was no more. Their sole desire was to have done with the war and go home. But they left behind them a world in which conquest and subjugation had become possible. And they inspired at least one empire – possibly, by virtue of the story's constant retelling, the greatest of them all. Plutarch, who has left us so vivid a psychological portrait of Alexander the Great, tells us that his copies of the *Iliad* and the *Odyssey* never left his side.[4] He slept with them, and a dagger, under his pillow.

The Homeric poems are mythic celebrations of the emergence of a people. Similar stories have been told about other places and other peoples at other times. They serve many roles. But they all celebrate the moment when a group acquires the means to impose itself upon its world. In the Mediterranean world this moment was made possible by the discovery and invention of hard resistant metals, bronze and later iron, which could be sharpened and would remain sharp. As many contemporary observers pointed out, it was not their firearms – which often did more harm to their users than to their intended victims – nor even their horses which allowed the

Spanish to defeat the Aztecs and the Incas. It was rather their steel weapons, weapons that had not changed substantially for centuries. Against these, the brittle obsidian axes of the Aztecs, which shattered or blunted after the first blow, could make little impact.

Together with the new instruments of war, there emerged also a new kind of combat. The heroes of the *Iliad* still fought as individuals seeking individual gains and, in Achilles' case, pursuing private feuds onto the battlefield. But among the Greek ranks, who are of scant interest to Homer, there is evidence of cohesion, of organization, of a terrifying sense of purpose, a willingness to surrender the moment in order to win the day. All of this the earlier warriors hordes lacked, as did their American, African or Australian counterparts. The Aztecs could never understand the kind of war that was being made against them. Even though they had secured some kind of tributary authority over a vast area of Central Mexico, they were more concerned with acquiring sacrificial victims – the traditional objective of Mesoamerican warfare – than defending a civilization that was about to be extinguished.[5] This was to be the final cause of their downfall and, in general, the weakness of all those, in other parts of the world, who would over the centuries by swept aside by the technologies and the sheer relentlessness of the European powers.

The war machine, the capacity to transform a large body of men into a single instrument of destruction, was to prove decisive in what has come to be called the 'triumph of the West'.[6] The image of the Athenian army, whose soldiers held a spear in their right hands and in their left a shield with which they covered not themselves but their neighbours, has long been used as an image of Attic democracy. And so it probably is. It is also, however, an image of the people as an army. Each man shelters and is sheltered by his neighbour. The survival of one depends upon the survival of the whole. Cowardice or desertion could lead only to immediate destruction of the entire unit. The Greeks, and later the Romans, were good at this sort of thing. The Greek phalanx, particularly after the reforms of Philip II of Macedon in about 356 BC, was capable of organizing the resources of thousands of trained infantry, in conjunction with equally skilled cavalry regiments, into a solid compact fighting force more formidable than anything that could be pitched against them.

The person who benefited most from these new technologies of power, who used them to create what has since antiquity been looked upon as the first of the great European empires, was Alexander the Great.

During its relatively brief existence, from 336 until 323 BC, Alexander's empire was the most extensive the ancient world had ever seen. Although it did not last long, it transformed the world in ways that were to have immense consequences for the subsequent history of all the peoples of Europe. Alexander destroyed the great Achaemenid Persian empire which had been a constant threat to the cities of Greece since Xerxes' attacks on Athens in 480 BC. He united, if only briefly, vast regions of what we now call Europe and Asia. He also succeeded in uniting the quarrelsome independent Greek states. In doing so, however, he deprived them not only of their independence but also of their unique, democratic forms of government. Henceforth, until its resurgence in the late eighteenth century, the rule of the many would, ultimately, surrender to the rule of the one.

Alexander had been, if only briefly, the pupil of Aristotle who, with Plato, had created not only European philosophy but many of the natural sciences as well. In his *Politics* Aristotle had argued that in the ideal state a mixed constitution, one that combined democracy, aristocracy and monarchy, would be best. But he also knew that ideal states existed only in the imagination. In the real world he inhabited, a world dominated by the experience of civil war and inter-city conflict, monarchy was much to be preferred. This was one lesson from his old tutor which Alexander had taken to heart. The various leagues of the Greek city-states had ultimately proved to be ineffective against Persian aggression. As Cyrus the Great, the architect of the Achaemenid empire, is said to have remarked of the Spartans, 'I never yet feared men who have a place demarcated in their city in which to meet and deceive each other on oath!' In Persian eyes, talk, and the lies upon which the democratic assemblies of the people thrived, would always weaken the Greeks' powers of decision. Cyrus, of course, underestimated Sparta. But Greece was ill-equipped to defeat a consolidated monarchy. As early as the sixth century BC, the philosopher Thales of Miletus had suggested that the only way to resist the Persians was to transform the loose-knit alliances of the city-states into a true federal state with a council at Teos. No one, however, had paid any attention to him. The Greek states became progressively less able to resist outside aggression, so that by 346 the Athenian orator Isocrates was able to describe Thebes, Argos, Sparta and Athens – the once-great cities of the Greek world – as all equally 'reduced to a common level of disaster'. In the end it took a monarch to destroy the might of the Persian king of kings.

Alexander did not, however, create his vast empire entirely on his own. Much of what he achieved had already been prepared for him by his father Philip II (382–336 BC). It was he who had transformed Macedon from a kingdom divided by civil war and foreign intervention into the most powerful of the Greek states. It was he who had created the seemingly invincible Macedonian army which at Chaeronea in August 338 won a crushing victory over an alliance of southern Greek cities led by Athens and Thebes. Philip's forces on that occasion are said to have numbered 30,000 foot and 2000 horse, a staggering number at a time when the adult male population of Sparta has been estimated at less than one thousand. The battle of Chaeronea made Philip the effective master of the Greek world and Macedon an unchallenged superpower. Philip then turned his attention to the already weakened Persian empire. In 336 a Macedonian expeditionary force of 10,000 men began the subjugation of the coast of Asia Minor. Philip, however, never lived to complete his conquest. As with so many rulers in the ancient world, he fell victim to an assassin.

Two years later, Alexander, who had inherited both his father's throne and his ambition, crossed the Hellespont, determined to put an end to Persian power for ever. His army, the largest ever to leave Greek soil, numbered 43,000 foot, armed with fearsome pikes six metres long, and 5500 horse. The cities of the Achaemenid empire, Sardis, Ephesus, Miletus, Phaselis, Aspendus and the Phrygian city of Gordian, fell one after another. At Gordian, Alexander paused long enough to perform one of those symbolic acts the memory of which has survived long after his conquest. In the ancient palace of Phrygian kings he was shown the legendary wagon of Gordius, the mythical founder of the dynasty. The yoke of the wagon was fastened to its pole by an elaborate knot the ends of which were invisible. Legend had it that anyone who was able to untie the Gordian knot would become lord of Asia. Alexander did not bother trying to undo the knot; he simply took out his sword and cut it. For later historians this act became a sign of divine endorsement for the entire campaign, and 'cutting the Gordian knot' has remained a metaphor for decisive action, and a presage of empire, until this day.

In the early winter of 333 Alexander defeated the vast Persian army at Issus, which gave him control of what is now the Near East as far as the Euphrates. He then moved into Egypt and Mesopotamia and finally in the winter of 331–330 seized the Persian capital at Persepolis. Until this time Alexander had been relatively constrained in his handling of defeated populations. But his men were growing restless, eager to lay their hands on some of the booty they had been promised. Persepolis was turned over to the victorious army. The houses of the nobility were looted, the men slaughtered and the women enslaved. Some months later, after an orgiastic banquet, and urged on by the courtesan Thaïs (later to become the wife of Ptolemy), Alexander and his entourage burned down the great palace of the Persian king of kings. It was, or so the Greek historians claimed, the final act of revenge for Xerxes' despoliation of the Acropolis in Athens.

Alexander then marched eastwards to consolidate his hold over the empire. Moving in a great swathe through what is now eastern Iran and western Afghanistan he crossed the Hindu Kush and invaded Bactria in the spring of 329. Here, however, his empire finally reached its limit. In 326 his troops, soaked

and exhausted by monsoon rains and faced by an enemy equip-
ped with elephant squadrons of legendary strength, refused to
cross the Beas river which separated them from the lands of the
Ganges. Like Achilles, his favourite Homeric hero, Alexander
retreated to his tent and for three days nursed his anger, waiting
for a change of heart. It did not come. Finally he made the
regular sacrifice for a river crossing and the omens proved,
conveniently, to be most inauspicious. Now that he could interpret his retreat as a concession not to his men but to the will of
the gods, he agreed to turn back.

Alexander returned to Persepolis and then moved to Babylon
where he began to prepare for the invasion of the Persian Gulf
and the Arabian littoral. For this he created a new army (one
less likely to challenge his ambitions) and a new navy. But
they were never put to the test. Towards the end of May 323
Alexander attended a banquet and, if the traditional accounts
are to believed, literally drank himself to death. The climax
came in an exchange of toasts in which he is said to have downed
twelve pints of undiluted wine in one steady draught. He
doubled up with a violent spasms and collapsed into a coma
from which his doctors were unable to revive him.[7]

This, briefly, is Alexander's story. In most senses it is exemplary. Like most empire-builders Alexander took over an earlier
and already weakened power. Although he moved large numbers
of Greek settlers into Persia, he did very little to alter the
administrative structure of the Persian empire. He ruled through
'satraps' – a Persian word meaning 'defenders of power' – as the
Persians themselves had done and, indeed, as most later empire-
builders, from the Romans to the British, were to do. In many
places, such as Sardes, the centre of Persian rule in Asia Minor,

he appointed his own men. In others he merely replaced local princes who had been loyal to the previous regime with ones of his own choosing.

Alexander's rule was always a personal one. At the centre of the empire was the figure and the legend of Alexander himself. He built up around him an elaborate court, something that had been largely absent from the traditional Greek *polis*. He invented a royal diadem, part Macedonian, part Persian in design, and even created a distinctive hairstyle for himself – the famous *anastole*, a quiff thrown back from a central parting. To ensure that all of this would survive him, he decreed that only one painter, one sculptor and one maker of medals – all men whom he could trust to produce the most flattering likenesses – were to be allowed to preserve his image.[8]

Like most rulers in the ancient world Alexander believed himself to be descended from semi-divine beings, from Andromache and Achilles on his mother's side and from Hercules on his father's. The final tribute that a man could pay to himself, however, was divinity itself. On a visit to the shrine of the god Ammon in the Libyan oasis of Siwah, Alexander told the chronicler Callisthenes that he had been greeted by the god as his son, and requested that after his death his body be taken to Siwah for burial. Ammon may have been Libyan by origin, but the Egyptians recognized in him the ram-god Amun and the Greeks, settled in nearby Cyrene, knew him as Zeus. It was characteristic of Alexander that he should have chosen as his divine parent not only the deity who had fathered Perseus and Hercules but also one who belonged to both the cultures, the East and the West, that he had hoped to unify.

An empire that was associated so clearly with the personal

authority and the carefully nurtured image of a single individual could not survive his death for long. Even in the final years of his life, Alexander was facing a mutiny of the Macedonian troops, a rising of the Greek settlers in Bactria, and imminent war in Greece itself. When he died his empire in effect died with him. He had appointed no heir and had no obvious successor. After a series of bloody civil wars the empire was divided up among his former generals. Even Macedon itself, weakened by Alexander's constant demand for manpower, was no longer able to dictate terms to the rest of the Greek world. In time the whole of Alexander's former domains would be overrun by another, greater imperial power: Rome.

For centuries, Alexander had been the archetypal empire-builder. 'The sole conqueror in the memory of mankind to have founded a universal empire,' enthused the Latin novelist Apuleius[9] – a model to be followed and an example to be surpassed. Julius Caesar tells how he wept when reading the history of Alexander, for 'Alexander had died at the age of thirty-two, king of so many peoples, while he himself had not achieved any brilliant success.' Some version of this story was repeated by both Pompey and Marc Antony (Pompey went so far as to copy Alexander's hairstyle, adopt the sobriquet 'the Great' and encourage his panegyrists to exaggerate his youth during his conquests of Judaea and Syria),[10] the emperor Trajan, Napoleon, and no doubt countless other would-be imperialists.[11] Nor was Alexander's image confined to the Western world. 'Sikander' became for generations of Persian monarchs a model of the world ruler, and in some accounts the precursor of the universal kingdom of Islam which would one day encompass the globe. 'My name is Shah Ismail,' wrote the founder of the Safavid dynasty in one of his self-aggrandizing poems, 'I am the living Khizr, and Jesus son of Mary, / I am the Alexander of my contemporaries.'

Alexander became 'the Great', however, not only because of his astonishing military successes. He became great for another more immediately modern reason. According to Plutarch, Aristotle had advised Alexander to treat only Greeks as human beings and to look upon all the other peoples he conquered as either animals or plants. This advice Alexander wisely ignored, for had he accepted his mentor's council he would have 'filled his kingdoms with exiles and clandestine rebellions'.[12] This anecdote is an allusion to the widespread Greek distinction between themselves and those whom they called 'barbarians'. The word 'barbarian' (*barbaros*) described all those who could not speak Greek and whose languages sounded, to Greek ears, merely like people stuttering 'bar bar'. Since only the Greeks had articulate speech only the Greeks were truly human. All the rest were, indeed, only animals or plants. For this reason, said Euripides (quoted approvingly by Aristotle) 'it is fit that the Greeks should rule over the barbarians'.[13] It had been this division of humankind and all that it implied which, in Kant's view, had been the cause of the ultimate collapse of Hellenic civilization. Alexander's vision of a universal empire was an explicit rejection of any such xenophobia. His ambition had been not merely to conquer or even to assimilate the mighty Persian empire, but to unite East and West, Asia and Europe, Hellene and barbarian. In this way he would be remembered not as a conqueror at all but, in Plutarch's words, 'as one sent by the gods to be the conciliator and arbitrator of the Universe'.[14] He had hoped that in his empire the old enmity between East and West – the origins of which are to be found in the myth of the Rape of Europa, an Asian princess abducted to Western shores, and in the story of the Trojan War, a struggle over a Western woman abducted to Eastern shores – would finally be brought to a close.

He did not, of course, succeed. But his image lived on after him on both sides of the Hellespont. In one Persian version of the Alexander legend, he is said to have erected a giant copper wall at the very edge of the world to protect the whole of 'civilization' from Gog and Magog, the twin giants which embody all that is untamed and inhuman.

Alexander's vision of empire, or at least the vision that later historians have attributed to him, had many of the properties which later empires would claim for themselves, from ancient Rome to the United States: the capacity to provide a living space for diverse peoples, to create peace and order in a world which would otherwise be at war with itself, and to defend a tenuous, hard-won and fragile civilization against all that might threaten it. The realities behind the legend were certainly very different. But that is unimportant; Alexander's greatness lies less in what he intended to achieve than in what he was believed to have achieved. It is for that reason that he has been looked upon by subsequent generations as the first world conqueror.

Alexander is a good starting point for our story for another reason. More than any other would-be world-ruler, his life became a tale of the elision of knowledge and understanding with power, of the merging of science and exploration with domination and settlement. It is doubtful if the real Alexander, despite his much publicized devotion to Homer, was overly concerned with learning, and despite his tutelage at the hands

of Aristotle the science to which he could have been exposed
was necessarily limited and in its infancy. Hostile later com-
mentators such as the Greek comic dramatist Menander
represented him as a drunkard, and the Roman philosopher
Seneca called him 'swollen beyond the limits of human arro-
gance', unedifying, intemperate and wild.[15] But by the time
Arrian in the second century AD sat down to write the history
of his life, Alexander had already become a figure possessed not
merely of the ability to conquer but also of an insatiable desire
for knowledge. It was, or so legend had it, for Alexander that
Aristotle had written not only the first treatise on politics but
also one of the earliest studies of astronomy.

In the Middle Ages, this Alexander became a legendary figure
whose desire to subjugate the entire world was matched only
by his ambition to know all its secrets and visit all its parts.
Stories were told of his quest for the hidden sources of the Nile,
of his invention of a diving bell to reach the floor of the ocean,
and of a great basket drawn by griffins in which he attempted
to reach Heaven.[16] In the Persian, Indian and later Ottoman
versions of his life he became a prophet, a seer, and – like
Gilgamesh, the hero of a cycle of poems from Mesopotamia
dating from the third millennium BC – a seeker after eternal
life. In Walter of Châtillon's poem *Alexandreis*, which dates
from the twelfth century, he is described as 'the prince who had
called the earth too narrow and prepared armed throngs to lay
open her secret parts', lines which run together in one erotic
image both the conqueror's desire to possess and the scientist's
desire to know. This Alexander, like the figure of Ulysses whom
Dante meets in Hell (and who is given many of Alexander's
attributes), tries to sail beyond the Pillars of Hercules and

dreams of conquering the western sun.[17] The greatest empire-builder in the history of Europe thus becomes also its greatest explorer, traveller and seeker after truth.

2   The empire of the Roman people

In the end, Alexander himself might not have succeeded in holding together Europe and Asia. Their enmities survived him, and have lasted to this day, as the Ottoman Turks and then the Russians replaced the Persians, and as first the Romans and then the Christian Latin kingdoms of Europe replaced the Greeks. But something of Alexander's image of empire and his ambitions have remained: the wish to bring peace, stability, religious and cultural harmony, and ultimately to unite under one rule all the peoples of world.

Alexander created what has been looked upon since antiquity as the first European empire. Its successor in nearly every respect was Rome. Rome has consistently provided the inspiration, the imagery and the vocabulary for all the European empires from early modern Spain to late nineteenth-century Britain. All the former imperial capitals of Europe – London, Vienna, Berlin – are filled with grandiose architectural reminders of this indebtedness to Rome. Even the United States, which was created out of the dismemberment of one kind of empire and has throughout the course of its history done its best to avoid assuming the role of another, is ruled from a city that was built to replicate as far as possible parts of ancient Rome. No other modern nation is governed from a building called the Capitol.

Rome began sometime during the seventh century BC as a small city-state of farmers and tradesmen occupying a territory of a few square miles on the lower Tiber. Its original rulers had been kings, like those of the neighbouring peoples, the Sabines, the Etruscans, the Latins and the Umbrians. By the late sixth century, however, Rome had become a republic although, unlike the Greek city-states on which it was loosely modelled, it was in no sense a democracy.

Alexander's example, and that of the Achaemenid empire which he defeated, might seem to suggest that all truly successful empires have been monarchies. The early history of Rome, however, demonstrates that although most empires have in time succumbed to some kind of monarchical rule, as did Rome itself, there has never been any reason why a republic could not also be an empire. Republics, after all, are no more given to caring for the rights or the lives of others than are monarchies. Neither are republics any less expansive, or less concerned with glory, than monarchies. Those who are 'citizens' might enjoy more freedom and, in theory at least, have a greater say in the business of government than those who are mere 'subjects'. But those who live outside, who are neither fellow-citizens nor fellow-subjects, are quite as vulnerable to republicans as they are to monarchists.

Throughout European history expansion has generally been popular with the majority of the people, so long as it is going well and does not involve too onerous a tax burden. The empire of the Roman republic might have benefited most directly the patricians, the consuls and proconsuls who commanded the legions and whose power and wealth derived from their success in battle. But it had always been presented to the common people, the plebeians, as *their* empire, 'the empire of the people of Rome'. And, until the end, when the senate had long since ceased to wield political power, the legions of the empire still marched under the banner of the 'Senate and the People of Rome'. Scipio Africanus, a man who played an enduring role in much Roman history, was once accused by Naevius, the tribune of the senate, of accepting bribes from the Seleucid emperor Antiochus. It was a very serious charge. It was also an offence against Scipio's honour, a slur against his standing with the people. And it was to the people he turned. 'This,' he declared to the crowd which had gathered to hear him judged, 'is the anniversary of the great battle on African soil in which I defeated Hannibal, the Carthaginian, the most determined enemy of *your empire*.' Pointing at Naevius, he added, 'Let us not be ungrateful to the gods. Let us have done with that wretch and offer thanks to Jove.' He then walked to the Capitol. The crowd followed him and Naevius found himself alone. An invocation of the greatness of the empire had the power to make the people forget the petty misdemeanours of their rulers.[1]

The Romans, like the Macedonians before them, were highly skilled tacticians and military innovators. They were also thorough and ruthless. 'Virtue' – a word that derives from *vir*, the Latin word for 'man' – meant only courage in battle. This they possessed in abundance. By 272 BC they had already taken control of the Italian peninsula. They then moved overseas, first to Sicily and Carthage, a Phoenician colony which at the time occupied much of the hinterland of north and central Tunisia, and then into the eastern Mediterranean. By the first century BC most of what had survived of the empire of Alexander the Great had fallen into Roman hands. Roman armies put an end to the crumbling Macedonian monarchy at Pydna in 168 BC and destroyed Corinth in 146. The kingdoms of Macedonia, Asia and Syria now became Roman provinces. Egypt became a Roman protectorate, as did the vassal monarchies of the once vast Seleucid empire. The entire Mediterranean became a Roman lake: *mare nostrum*, 'our sea', as it came to be called. Most of what today is thought of as the Roman empire had been acquired under the republic. Britain, Dacia to the east of the Danube, Arabia, Mesopotamia and Armenia were taken by the emperors (most, with the exception of Britain, by Trajan between AD 101 and 117). But the full force of Roman expansion had stopped by the time Julius Caesar seized effective control of the senate in the first century BC. As the eighteenth-century English radical Richard Price sourly observed of his countrymen's self-serving idolization of the Roman republic, it had been 'nothing but a faction against the general liberties of the world'.[2]

The collapse of the republic and the creation of the principate were the outcome of what all empires have feared most: civil war. For if republics have been able to create empires, they have all sooner or later fallen prey to the ambitions of the strongest among them. This is what became of the Greek city-states, and it is what finally became of Rome when the empire had grown too big for the senate to able to control the army and the overweening ambitions of the mightiest of its generals. 'The empire of the Romans,' wrote the great eighteenth-century historian Edward Gibbon, 'filled the world, and when that empire fell into the hands of a single person, the world became a safe and dreary person for his enemies.'

The first of those men was Julius Caesar. Caesar had conquered Gaul in a spectacular if brutal campaign in 58 to 51 BC.

In 52 Pompey, who as sole consul was in effective control of the senate, fearful of Caesar's growing power and obvious autocratic ambitions, attempted to prevent him from returning to Rome as consul. Caesar's response was to invade Italy. Pompey had some initial success but was finally defeated near Pharsalus in Thessaly in 48. Caesar now proclaimed himself dictator (an office generally assumed only at moments of crisis and for a limited duration) and consul for life. He also adopted the style and dress of the old Roman kings (although he refused the title *rex*) and after much bullying succeeded in having himself declared a god. The republic had become in all but name a monarchy. On 15 March 44, he was stabbed to death on the steps of the senate, in what is probably one of the most celebrated assassinations in European history, by a motley group of 'republicans' and ex-Pompeians led by Brutus and Cassius, two of his former companions. Caesar's death did nothing to restore the republic as his assassins had hoped. Instead, it plunged the Roman world into a civil war which nearly destroyed the empire, something that no later Roman would ever forget.

Caesar's name has supplied the title for autocratic rulers of one kind or another until the twentieth century, the last being Tsar ('Caesar') Alexander of Russia. In fact, despite his openly despotic behaviour he did little to change the republican constitution of Rome beyond grafting his divine and hereditary rule onto it. It was his successor Octavian who in 27 BC had the title Augustus ('revered one') conferred upon himself, who was the first to adopt the term Emperor (*Imperator*) as a title, and who was the ideological and institutional founder of what is now called the principate, the period in the history of the empire when it was in effect ruled by one man. It was Augustus who succeeded in bringing the civil war to an end, brought peace to the empire and established a centralized system of government. He reined in the power of local aristocrats, deprived the senate and the people of most of their authority, and reformed and hugely extended the rule of law.[3]

Augustus also radically overhauled the tax system, on which his ability to pay his troops depended. Previously, cash flows to the treasury had been erratic and uncertain. Now the whole Roman world was enrolled and a census was held of every potential contributor. One of the unintended consequences of this new fiscal order was the journey of an obscure Judaean carpenter named Joseph and his pregnant wife to be registered at the town of Bethlehem. As Christian historians would repeat over and over, it was no accident of history that Augustus' new order should have come into being at the same moment as the birth of the man whose teaching would usher in another and, in their eyes, final, God-ordained, world order. God had sent Augustus to unite the world and, in doing so, to prepare the way for the coming of Christ.

Augustus also presided over the Golden Age of Latin literature, the age of the epic poet Virgil, whose *Aeneid*, a celebration of the origins of Rome, became for the Roman people something similar to what the *Iliad* and the *Odyssey* had been for the Greeks. It was the age, too, of Ovid (although Augustus banished him to Tomis on the Black Sea, probably because of his part in some scandal involving the imperial house), whose writings have had more impact on later European literature than perhaps any other classical author, as well as of the poets Horace, Tibullus and Propertius, and the historian Livy. In their different ways all of these writers celebrated the greatness, past, present and to come, of the new Roman order. Augustus thus became a hero who over the centuries would be venerated by pagan and Christian alike; and, like Caesar and the title of Emperor, the name of Augustus was also adopted by later princes with aspirations to empire. 'Most invincible Caesar and August Emperor ...' began one version of the roll-call of titles of the Holy Roman Emperor Charles V.

To its citizens, Rome offered some measure of protection, a way of life that, for better or for worse, we have come to call 'civilized', and membership of the greatest state the Western world had ever known. To the patrician classes it offered, too, the prospect of wealth and, more importantly, glory. Glory is the desire for the esteem and admiration of others. In the ancient world, and indeed in most worlds until perhaps very recently, the most obvious and in some cases the only field in which it could easily be won was the field of battle. The orator, jurist and philosopher Marcus Tullius Cicero (106–43 BC) even looked upon what he described as 'fighting for empire and seeking glory' as a particular kind of warfare. It was, he said, one that was 'waged less bitterly' than war for 'defence or restitution' since what was at stake here was not who would survive but who would rule.[4] A man might be praised or admired, or loved, for being a just and benign ruler, but glory was an altogether noisier, flashier and ultimately more deadly affair. The people, wrote the sixteenth-century Italian political philosopher Giovanni Botero, reflecting on the lessons to be learned from Rome's history, will always prefer a strong, irascible and triumphant ruler to a wise and prudent one, just as they 'prefer a tumbling torrent to a calm river'.[5]

Glory-seeking strategists carried the Roman empire, just as they had the Macedonian monarchy. Empire was about the rewards to be had from war, and as it grew the Roman empire increasingly became less a people with a standing army than a population in arms, a military culture which embraced the entire free male population. By the time imperial rule had been fully established under Augustus, what the Romans referred to as the *domi*, that which pertains to the home, or what today we would 'civil society', had been virtually subsumed into the military, the *militae*. Towards the end, Roman society became a world in which scribes were soldiers, bishops were soldiers, local governors were soldiers, and, of course, the emperor was a soldier. Ultimately this was to become not only the source of Rome's greatness, but also, as Edward Gibbon recognized, the cause of its downfall. Later imperial cultures from sixteenth-century Spain to twenty-first-century America, with their far greater social complexity, would learn to distinguish more clearly between civil and military power and to ensure the subservience of the latter to the former. Yet the office of the president of the United States still combines supreme, if also highly restricted, command over the military as well as the civil sphere, as the French monarchy did in its time and in theory at least the British monarch (who biannually dispenses honours in the name of the now vanished British empire) does to this day.

Rome's greatness was not, however, built on military might alone. The more extended the empire and the greater the distance, both geographically and politically, between the centre and the periphery, the more difficult the task of governance becomes. Even modern societies, with all the immense power available to the state, can only be ruled for prolonged periods of time with the consent of their members – as numerous auto-crats, both ancient and modern, have discovered to their cost. 'It is on opinion only that government is founded,' wrote the philosopher David Hume in the eighteenth century. And what is true of all governments is especially so of those that seek to unite a diversity of peoples with a variety of expectations, customs, beliefs, and loyalties.

If the empire was to outlast its founder and be proof against intruders, it had to have something to offer its conquered peoples, something that would persuade them that their way of life under the conqueror would be ultimately better than that which they had enjoyed before. It was not only Roman roads and Roman architecture, or even the much spoken of but not always so obvious *pax Romana*, which persuaded non-Roman patricians from North Africa to Scotland to identify themselves with the empire. It was the lure of luxury, opulence and the trappings of power. It had been precisely his encounter with the splendours of the doomed city of Ravenna, the glittering gilded domes, the opulent buildings with their arched and pillared porticoes, the symmetry and, even at this time of siege, the orderliness of its streets, the elaborate dress of its inhabitants, in particular the women with their stacked hair and tottering shoes – it had been this prospect of a life far richer than any the wandering Lombard warrior had experienced elsewhere that persuaded Droctulft that this was not something he could help to destroy.

The Roman empire thus constituted not only a state but a way of living, what Cicero identified as 'our wise grasp of a single truth'.[6] And it was embodied in that all-precious commodity, citizenship. To be a citizen, a *civis*, meant to be able to say, in that celebrated phrase, 'I am a Roman citizen' – *civis Romanus sum* – not a Gaul or a Spaniard or an Egyptian, but a Roman. It meant to belong to what was called the *civitas*, the Roman civil community, and the word from which the more ambiguous modern term 'civilization' derives. Above all, it meant, in a sense that the word has retained to this day, to live in a society which, for all its great injustices (by modern standards), was looked upon as the embodiment of the rule of law. To be a Roman citizen meant to acquire a legal identity and a place in a system of understanding and controlling human behaviour which was intended to extend over the entire planet.

Roman law became the law of the whole of Europe, and despite having been extensively modified by the legal customs of the Germanic tribes which overran the empire in the fifth century, it has remained the basis of most of our understanding of what law is until this day. It was the Romans' great intellectual achievement, as moral philosophy and the natural sciences had been that of the Greeks. For Roman jurists the law was the supreme expression of human rationality. 'However we may define man,' wrote Cicero, 'a single definition will apply to all ... For those creatures who have received the gift of reason from Nature have also received right reason, and therefore they have also received the gift of law ... And if they have received law they have received justice. Now all men have received reason; therefore all men have received justice.'[7]

The history of Roman law begins, in effect, with the Twelve Tables, said to have been composed between 451 and 450 BC. The effect of these was to ensure that henceforth all customary law would be given a legislative basis and enacted by statute. Later Roman jurists attempted to gather all these enactments together in series of codes, of which the most enduring was compiled under the Eastern emperor Justinian in the fifth century AD. Justinian's codification is divided into four books, running to over a million words: the *Codex*, the *Digest*, the *Pandect* and the *Institutes*. Like most legislators, Justinian hoped that his definition of the law would prove to be so authoritative that there would be no further need for lawyers to interpret it. He turned out, of course, to be wrong. His codification was only the beginning of a vast proliferation of later commentaries and interpretations which, from the eleventh century onwards, became the basis for all legal education and administration throughout Europe.

Roman law was predominantly civil law, which is to say that it was concerned with the laws governing the peoples of Rome and, as Rome spread, of the empire as a whole. But the Romans also created a legal category called the 'law of nations'. In practical terms this was that part of the Roman civil law that was open to Roman citizens and foreigners alike. In a wider sense, however, it was taken to be what the second-century jurist Gaius called 'the law observed by all nations'. This concept was to have a prolonged and powerful impact on all subsequent European legal thinking. As the European powers reached outwards into other areas of the globe, many of which the Romans had never imagined, it became the basis for what is now called 'public international law', and it still governs all the actions, in theory if not consistently in practice, of the 'international community'.

Roman law also introduced into Europe the crucial idea that warfare itself had to be regulated, and above all that wars could not be fought simply for personal gain. 'The imperial majesty,'

Justinian began his *Institutes*, 'should be armed with laws as well as glorified with arms.'[8] The Greeks, and their antagonists, had been largely unconcerned with the justice of war. When Alexander invaded the Persian empire he did so initially, he claimed, to avenge the wrongs committed by the Persians against the Greeks. But the territories he seized and attempted to Hellenize were what was called 'spear-won'. The conqueror's right to possession lay merely in his success in battle. The Romans, however, introduced a complex distinction, which still governs the conduct of most modern conflicts, between 'just' and 'unjust' wars.[9] In general, the Roman jurists looked upon war as a means of last resort, the objective of which must always be to acquire not cultural and religious transformation, much less territory, but peace and justice. Human beings, Cicero insisted, used language to resolve their differences and resorted to violence only when language had failed.[10] This was one of the things which distinguished them from mere brutes. A just war could only be waged defensively and in pursuit of compensation for some alleged act of aggression against either the Romans or their allies. 'The best state,' according to Cicero, 'never undertakes war except to keep faith or in defence of its safety.'[11] Most Romans, however, fully recognized that Rome, like the United States and the Soviet Union in the 1950s and 1960s, frequently acquired clients with the sole purpose of 'defending' them against enemies, real or imaginary, whose territories they wished to acquire. Neither did the doctrine of the just war prevent Roman warfare from being in reality spectacularly brutal. When the Romans sacked a city, observed Polybius, they were so ferocious that they even killed all the animals.

Ultimately, Roman law was intended not merely to create political and social order, but also to confer an ethical purpose upon the entire community. Under the late republic, and then more forcibly under the principate, the legal formulation of *imperium* merged with the Stoic ideal of a single universal human race, in Cicero's phrase 'a single joint community of gods and men'.[12] To be a member of the community meant to acquire an identity more enduring, more compelling than anything that the membership of a village or a tribe could confer. In the real world of ancient Rome, Astérix and his friends would have been a quaint anomaly with very little motive for continuing to resist the lure of Roman civilization. (True, the Isaurians, *montagnard* warriors from the Taurus, proved to be so indomitable that they were given their own frontier, yet even they, at the end of the fifth century, placed their own candidate, Zeno, on the imperial throne in Constantinople.) As James Wilson observed in 1790, as he mused upon the possible future of the United States as the new Rome in the West, 'It might be said, not that the Romans extended themselves over the whole globe, but that the inhabitants of the globe poured themselves upon the Romans.' This, he concluded, was clearly 'the most secure method of enlarging an empire'.[13]

Nearly three centuries earlier, an admiring Niccolò Machiavelli had observed that Rome had 'ruined her neighbours' and created a world empire in the process precisely by 'freely admitting strangers to her privileges and honours'. Compare, he went on, Rome with Sparta. Lycurgus, the legendary father of the Spartan republic, because he 'believed that nothing would more readily destroy its laws, did everything to prevent strangers from coming into the city'. As a consequence Sparta had slowly stagnated until it was forcibly incorporated into the Roman province of Achaea.[14]

Rome, by contrast, had flourished. By the time Augustus came to power, it had become in effect a huge cosmopolitan state. For its most skilful and fortunate subjects the empire was a vast resource, often more enriching than the narrow limits of the original communities from which they came. Peoples from all over the empire could be found in almost every Roman province. Even the emperors themselves, after the second and third centuries AD, were sometimes neither Roman nor even Italian, at least by birth: Septimus Severus was born in North Africa; Trajan, who took the empire to its furthermost limits, in Spain; and Diocletian in Dalmatia. In this way, Roman imperialism came to be seen not as a form of oppression, as the seizure by one people of the lands, the goods and the persons of others, but as a form of beneficent rule which involved not conquest but patronage, and the first purpose of which was the improvement of the lives of others. As Cicero also said of the imperial republic he served, 'We could more truly have been titled a protectorate [*patrocinium*] than an empire of the world.'[15]

When in AD 212 the emperor Caracalla granted citizenship to all the free inhabitants of the empire a common bond was created, at least in theory, which extended the Roman *civitas* to all the many peoples of which the empire was composed. 'Those within the Roman world,' declared the edict of Caracalla, 'have become Roman citizens.' From there it was but a brief step to declaring that Rome was the 'common homeland' of the entire world, and an even shorter step to declaring that those who were not citizens and showed no desire to become citizens should, if only in their own long-term interests, be obliged to do so. As Cicero had pointed out, even Africans, Spaniards and Gauls, 'savage and barbarous nations', were entitled to just government. If their own rulers were unable to provide it then the Romans would be happy to do so for them.

Like Alexander before them, the Roman rulers created an ideology which aimed at world domination. There were to be no limits to the rule of Rome – which is why, the historian Livy tells us, Terminus, the god of boundaries, had refused to be present at the birth of the city. Already by 75 BC coins were being struck with images of a sceptre, a globe, a wreath and a rudder, symbols of Rome's power over all the lands and oceans of the world. By the time Augustus came to power 'the World' – the *orbis terrarum* – and the empire had come to be identified as one. 'We look neither to this corner nor to that,' wrote the first-century playwright and philosopher Seneca, 'but measure the boundaries of our nation by the sun.'[16] When a century later the emperor Antoninus Pius took the title 'Lord of all the World' – *dominus totius orbis* – he was merely making explicit what all the Roman emperors had always assumed.

The Roman claim to rule the universe was not unique. Most rulers of very large areas of the world have aimed at one time or another at what they understood to be world domination. The Mughal emperors of northern India styled themselves 'Lords of the Universe'. The rulers of Vijayanagara, the 'City of Victory' on the Tungabhadra river in southern India, claimed 'to rule the vast world under a single umbrella'.[17] The Chinese emperor, the Huang Di, was the supreme lord of all humankind, for even if the Chinese knew full well that he did not literally rule over the entire world, all that he did was believed to affect even those who were not, or not yet, his subjects. The idea of Roman citizenship, however, expressed more than the exercise of simple power. It was about creating a world which would outlive even the empire itself. Even as Britain became independent, Gaul fell to usurpers, the Goths took possession of the Eternal City and the emperors in Ravenna (the city which would become a nemesis for Droctulft) began issuing laws to safeguard the Holy Roman and Catholic Church, the poet Claudian could still offer to the Teutonic vice-regent of the emperor Honorius (that 'pale flower of the women's quarters') lines in praise of universal citizenship: 'She [Rome] alone who has received the conquered into her bosom, and like a mother not an empress, protected the human race with a common name, summoning those whom she has defeated to share her citizenship.'[18]

Such sentiments would remain an aspiration of all later Western empires. As one British political philosopher expressed it in 1923, 'the thought on which the best of the Romans fed was a thought of a World-State, the universal law of nature, the brotherhood and the equality of men.'[19] This was meant to be as much a description of the British empire, at a time when it was still a going concern, as it was of the Romans. And some conception of universal citizenship has sustained every cry for justice, sincere or mendacious, that has ever been made in the name of 'humanity', 'mankind' or, more recently, that shifting and amorphous body, 'the international community'.

Until the late eighteenth century, however, 'the world' over which in their various ways its would-be rulers claimed sovereignty was an immense, uncertain place. In Cicero's *Scipio's*

Dream, which became one of the most popular accounts of the frightening infinitude of space, the Roman general Scipio Aemilianus has a dream in which he finds himself talking to his deceased adoptive grandfather, Scipio Africanus. Africanus takes him on a tour of the heavens, from where he is able to gaze down upon the earth.

> You see that the earth is inhabited in only a few portions, and those very small, while vast deserts lie between them ... You see that the inhabitants are so widely separated that there can be no communication whatever among the different areas; and that some of the inhabitants live in parts of the earth that are oblique, transverse and sometimes directly opposite your own, from such you can expect nothing surely that is glory. Examine this northern zone which you inhabit and you will see what a small portion of it belongs to you Romans. You cannot fail to see what a narrow territory it is over which your glory is so eager to spread.

In reality, the younger Scipio (as his adoptive grandfather is also made to predict) would go on to destroy Carthage in 146 BC, thus bringing the third Punic War to a victorious conclusion, and to take Numantia in northern Spain. But Scipio Africanus' vision of a vast, unknowable and ultimately unpossessable globe would remain to haunt the imagination not only of the Romans but of most subsequent would-be empire-builders in Europe. 'Empire', as Cicero knew, is about glory. And, as Africanus makes clear, if you cannot aspire to hold all of the world, it would be better to give up hope of any of it. Better to think about the pleasures of the afterlife or the things of the spirit which alone are of lasting value. For even, says Africanus, if what we achieve in our own lifetimes is glorious, 'even if future generations should wish to hand down to those yet unborn the eulogies of every one of us' – even then the disasters which overrun the world would prevent anyone 'from gaining a glory which would be long-enduring, much less eternal'.[20]

Cicero attributed these sentiments to one of the greatest of Roman generals, the man who, if Livy is to be believed, declared that 'The empire of the Roman people shall be extended to the furthest ends of the earth.'[21] Scipio Africanus may have been permitted to see how small his own triumphs had been when viewed from the heavens, and he may have come to the conclusion that his achievements, and those of all the other glory-seekers who have plagued the world, were ultimately illusory, grains of chaff in the wind. Cicero himself could certainly think that way. But Africanus' grandson was destined to go on in the same way, as was Rome itself, until it finally fell to other peoples with imperial ambitions.

For all Cicero's scepticism about the capacity of the Romans to occupy anything more than a very small portion of 'the world', the Roman empire was, before the arrival of the British in the nineteenth century, the most extensive in terms of inhabitable lands and population that the world had ever known. (The Russians, and before them the Mongols, ruled over more territory but most of it was unoccupied, and, prior to the development of modern technologies, largely unoccupiable.) At its height in the second century AD the Roman empire covered an area from the Atlas Mountains to Scotland and the Indus valley to the Atlantic, a territory of approximately five million square miles and a population which has been estimated at about fifty-five million. By one account, the process of expansion had only stopped when the Romans believed that they had reached the furthermost limits of what the Greeks called the *oikoumene*, the inhabitable world.[22] More prosaically, they stopped expanding when they reached the real limits of their capabilities, checked by the Parthians in the east and the vastness of the Atlantic Ocean in the west. By then, however, the empire had already become too large to be managed from a single centre, too diverse politically and culturally to sustain its claim to being a single state under a single rule of law.

In the end Rome fell prey to the limitlessness of its own ambitions. As the empire grew and the diversity of the peoples it included increased, so its sheer heterogeneity became more difficult to handle. Like all extensive empires it eventually reached a stage where it was no longer able to keep ahead of the competition and to satisfy its subject peoples.[23] Having reached a point of equilibrium in the second century, it began slowly but inexorably to be hollowed out from within as long-quiescent subject peoples revolted and once-loyal subjects seized the opportunity to carve out independent states for themselves. A similar fate befell the state of Vijayanagara in southern India, and the Muslim empires of the Ottomans, the Safavids and the Mughals. It is what became of Spain and Britain and, in its own way, the Soviet Union.

The dangers of overextension had been there since before the time of Augustus although no one had paid them much attention. Livy, writing in the early days of the principate, tells how, when Scipio Africanus took his army into Asia in 190 BC, he was met by Heraclides of Byzantium, ambassador of the Seleucid emperor Antiochus. Heraclides warned him to 'let the Romans limit their empire to Europe, that even this was very large; that it was easier to gain it part by part than to hold the whole'.[24] Scipio was unimpressed: 'What seemed to the ambassador great incentives for conducting peace,' commented Livy, 'seemed unimportant to the Romans.' Scipio marched on to begin what would be the final annexation of the empire of Alexander the Great. But Heraclides' words would return again and again to haunt not only later generations of Romans but most subsequent empire-builders.

By the end of the second century AD, the empire, as Heraclides predicted, had become impossible to hold together. Already, by 200, a serious trade recession had hit the Mediterranean. In the middle years of the century the Roman legions had suffered terrible defeats at the hands of Persians, Goths, and other Germanic tribes, and civil war had brought the imperial government to the verge of disintegration.[25] In a last attempt to keep it intact, the emperor Diocletian divided the empire into a Western and an Eastern half. The division was carried still further by his successor Constantine the Great, who in 324 created on the site of Byzantium on the shores of the Bosphorus a 'New Rome' for the Eastern empire and called it Constantinople, Greek for 'Constantine's city'.

In 312, at the battle of the Mulvian Bridge, Constantine had defeated his rival Maxentius for control of the entire empire. His victory, or so he later claimed, had come after he had seen in the sky a cross with the words 'Be victorious in this'. After his triumph, which later historians inevitably attributed to divine intervention, Constantine converted to Christianity, made it the official religion of the empire, and began the slow process of transforming a polytheistic pagan society into a monotheistic Christian one.[26] Henceforth the Roman empire, and with it the whole of what had now become Europe, acquired two separate identities: a Latin Western part, and a progressively Hellenized East which has come to be called the Byzantine empire. The latter remained until its end in 1453 the empire of the Romans, although by the fifth century it had become a Greek-speaking, wholly Hellenized culture. Roman culture under both the republic and the empire had always been heavily indebted to that of Greece. Men like Cicero, if never quite bilingual, had had Greek tutors and derived all of their philosophical training from Greek texts. Greek art, Greek architecture, Greek modes of dress and Greek ceremonial all left their mark on the Roman world. After the division of the empire Romans not only spoke two different languages, they adopted two distinct forms of Christianity: Greek Orthodoxy in the East and Catholicism in the West. In time these differences would deepen until finally any dialogue between the *basileus* in the East and the emperor in the West became impossible.

Byzantium outlived Rome. By the early years of the fifth century the empire in the West had been overrun by waves of Germanic tribes. In August 410, the traditional date for the formal end of the Roman empire in the West, the Eternal City was sacked and pillaged for three days by the armies of the Visigothic ruler Alaric. What remained of Rome revived briefly, but when in 476 the German Odoacer deposed the emperor Romulus Augustulus, the Western empire was finally extinguished.[27]

Byzantium, however, remained firmly in control of most of the East for another 500 years. In the eleventh century, however, Seljuk Turks seized Byzantine Armenia. In 1204 Constantinople itself fell to the marauding soldiery of the Fourth Crusade who held it until 1261. But it was the Ottoman Turks who were to carry out the final destruction of the Christian East. Beginning in the thirteenth century they moved steadily and inexorably westwards until in 1453, after a prolonged siege, Constantinople fell to the armies of Sultan Mehmet II, 'The Conqueror'. Thereafter it would become Istanbul and be rebuilt as the capital of another great power, the only Muslim empire the Christian world was ever prepared to accept as such. With the demise of the last Byzantine ruler, there would be 'two suns' shining upon the globe, two rulers competing for universal supremacy, a Christian emperor in the West and a Muslim sultan in the East.

3 Universal empire

The modern European world remains the heir to both of the civilizations of the ancient world. But with the final collapse of the Byzantine empire Greek culture was submerged for nearly 400 years. European society, despite its continuing indebtedness to Greek science and philosophy, became predominantly a Latin one on which the customs and languages of the Germanic invaders left deep and enduring marks. The former Roman *civitas* was transformed into a succession of fiefdoms, principalities, duchies, city-states and bishoprics. In time, all that remained of the status of the ancient Roman *imperium* belonged to the pope. The pope was the titular head of a secular state which was limited to southern and central Italy. But he was also the leader of a religious community which had always claimed that one day it would cover the entire globe – and this, as we shall see, was to have some far-reaching implications for subsequent relationships between the European imperial powers.

In 800 Pope Leo III, in the name of the people and city of Rome, conferred upon Charles I, the king of the Lombards and the Franks, who was subsequently known as Charlemagne (742–814), the title of Emperor. Between 771 and 778, Charlemagne had made himself sole ruler of the once-divided Frankish peoples, conquered the Lombard kingdom, and subdued and

Christianized the tribes of what is today Lower Saxony and Westphalia. He was a very long way from restoring the former Roman *imperium*, even within the traditional frontiers of Europe. But he had done more than any previous ruler. The new emperor was, as all his predecessors since Constantine had been, the defender of the church. He was the 'second sword' – the pope still wielded the first – of all Christendom. In 1157, in recognition of this role, Frederick I added the word Sanctus to his title and the empire thus became not merely Roman but also Holy.

Charlemagne's success in reuniting at least some of the many peoples which the dissolution of the Roman world had scattered into different communities did not, however, last for long. By 924 the Carolingian empire had been dissolved in Italy, and both France and Germany were in the process of becoming separate kingdoms. For Rome's true successor in the West was not to be yet another empire but instead a number of different kingdoms. By the mid-twelfth century each of the kings of Europe was claiming to be an emperor in his own kingdom, and what remained of the empire itself was gradually confined to the Germanic kingdoms. There it would remain, as Voltaire sarcastically remarked, 'neither Holy nor Roman nor an empire', for another 700 years until it was brought to an end by Napoleon in August 1806.

For most of the empire's long history, the Holy Roman emperors were princes who used their status to maintain an uneasy peace between the various political groups – free and imperial towns, landgraves and dukes, princes and prince-bishops, and the footloose Free Imperial Knights – which ruled over the German lands. (On the eve of the Reformation there were about 300 such political powers which were of real significance, and a host more which were not but believed themselves to be.) The emperor was, in that time-hallowed Latin phrase, *primus inter pares* – 'first amongst equals'. He was also, after the Frankish custom, not an hereditary but an elected ruler. By the fifteenth century, however, the imperial crown had become effectively hereditary within the Austrian Habsburg family, and with their ever-increasing power some of the real independence of the German princes began steadily to be eroded.

The ruler who did most to reassert the power of the empire and briefly transformed it from a merely German affair back into a true *imperium* was Charles V (1500–58). Charles had inherited from his grandfather Maximilian I most of what is now central and eastern Europe, and the Duchy of Burgundy which then included modern Holland and Belgium. He had inherited from his maternal grandparents, Ferdinand of Aragon and Isabella of Castile, the kingdoms of Spain, Castile and Aragon, and the Aragonese empire in Italy and the eastern Mediterranean. More significantly for the future of all the European states, he had also acquired a vast and as yet largely unexplored territory in the Western hemisphere, then known simply as the Indies.

When Charles of Burgundy, as he then was, set sail from the port of Flushing in Zeeland in September 1517 to claim the thrones of Castile and Aragon, the ship that carried him had painted on its sails an emblem depicting the Pillars of Hercules encircled with a banner nearing the legend *Plus Oultre*, 'further beyond'. The Pillars of Hercules was the name given to Mount Hacho and the Rock of Gibraltar, on the African and European sides of the Straits of Gibraltar. Legend had it that they had been set down to mark the limits of the known world and inscribed upon them had been the words *ne plus ultra*, 'no further beyond'. Beyond, for the ancients who knew nothing of oceanic navigation, lay only what the Arabs would later call the Green Sea of Darkness, which swallowed every vessel that dared to venture into it. Charles's removal of the word 'no' was an assertion made in the future tense. It was both a declaration that his empire had already passed the limits of that of Augustus, whose name he would later assume, and a statement about the further possibilities that were open to him.

According to the mythic genealogy which the eulogists of the house of Habsburg had provided for him, Charles had inherited his empire from Aeneas, Augustus and Constantine the Great, via Charlemagne.[1] It was an unbroken line which reached all the way back to the fall of Troy. The history of Rome, wrote the sixteenth-century Spanish imperial historian Pedro de Mexia, was the history of an empire which in 'longevity, size and power' was the greatest of all empires because it had begun 'a little less than 2300 years ago and is still alive today'.[2] Charles would complete the task which his ancestor, whose name he bore, had begun and reunite the whole of Europe under a single ruler. Moreover, the emblem of the Pillars proclaimed, he would go further than Caesar and Augustus. He would literally go forward and conquer the entire world. He himself, it must be said, claimed never to have harboured any such ambitions. In 1535, as suspicion of his intentions mounted, particularly in France, he went so far as to declare publicly before Pope Pius III that he had no aspirations whatsoever for universal empire. Not many, however, perhaps least of all the pope, ever wary of the objectives of the second sword of Christendom, believed him.

Charles' empire was not a single *imperium* but a vast,

sprawling, cosmopolitan conglomerate ruled over by an emperor who had no established capital, travelled ceaselessly to be with his loyal subjects, and tried to maintain the illusion, in the words of one seventeenth-century Milanese, that the ruler who held all these disparate realms together 'was only the king of each one of them'. Charles' empire resembled a modern multinational corporation more than a state. Although it was governed in accordance with an overarching legal principle, the imperial public law (*ius publicum*), it had no common legal system and no single administrative structure. It did not even have a single language. There is a woodcut by Albrecht Altdorfer which shows Maximilian I quelling a mutiny among his polyglot troops by addressing each one in his own tongue. Charles himself was said to have spoken Spanish to God, French to his mistress and German to his horse. Under the aegis of the emperor all his subjects supposedly enjoyed the same status whether they were Spanish, Walloons, Flemings, Neapolitans or even American Indians. God, wrote the sixteenth-century Italian poet Ludovico Ariosto, had willed it that 'under this emperor there should be only one flock and only one pastor', an inescapable allusion to St John's Gospel. For this reason making war on the Indians, declared the Spanish theologian Francisco de Vitoria in 1534, was making war not 'against strangers' but against vassals of the emperor 'as if they were natives of Seville'. Milanese, Florentines and Genoese settled in Spanish Naples and prospered there, acquiring Neapolitan lands and Neapolitan titles. Germans ran the printing presses of Seville, and Spaniards settled in the Netherlands (before the Dutch threw them out).

Charles' cosmopolitanism and claims to universalism were matched only by the rulers of the remainder of what had once been the ancient Hellenic and Roman worlds: the Ottoman empire (the Habsburg empire's immediate rival) and, further to the east the Safavid and Mughal empires. These were, if anything, even more porous than their Christian counterpart. The intelligentsia and guardians of the faith of the Muslim world shared a common body of texts: the Qur'an, the *Hadith* or traditions of the prophet, and the vast body of Arabic writings on philosophy and science which had been responsible for the diffusion of much Greek science, including most of Aristotle, into the Western world. Arabic and Persian were *linguae francae*, understood in educated circles at least from Budapest to Chittagong. Gujarati Hindus, Syrian Muslims, Jews, Armenians, and Christians from south and central Europe operated trading routes which supplied Persian and Arab horses to the armies of all three empires, Mocha coffee to Delhi and Belgrade, and Persian silk to India and Istanbul.[3] Arching over this international community and economy was the law of Islam which, like the *pax Romana*, offered considerable benefits to those who were prepared to accept the limitations it inevitably imposed.

All of these states saw themselves as heirs to the ancient empires which had preceded them. But the Habsburg empire was unlike both its Muslim rivals and its Roman and Greek predecessors in one crucial respect. All previous European and Asian empires – from those of the Medes and Achaemenids in Iran and the Ch'in in China, Vijayanagara in southern India, the empires of Alexander the Great, Genghis Khan, Tamburlaine, Caesar and Augustus, right up to the empire of Charles' paternal grandfather Maximilian – had been linked to large, well-trained and highly mobile land forces. They comprised territorial land-masses embracing myriad peoples and reaching over thousands of miles, but they were unbroken by large expanses of ocean. Charles' empire was also still land-based. It included most of central and eastern Europe, the Spanish kingdoms of Castile and Aragon, a large portion of southern Italy, the Duchy of Milan, and what are now Holland and Belgium. The greater part of it, however, at least as far as territory was concerned, lay overseas in America. And from the late fifteenth century on, the direction of European expansion would be increasingly maritime.

4 *Conquering the ocean*

In *Scipio's Dream* Cicero had created a vision of the real world, or at least of the world as Cicero thought it might be. Just how large that world was and just how many peoples it might contain was, of course, unknown. It was and would remain, until at least the late eighteenth century for most Europeans and well beyond for many others, a place of vertiginous geographical uncertainty. The Romans, the Mughals or the Chinese, even the Spanish and the Ottomans, all had very different visions of the planet from one another and from the one we have today. Maps were crude, inaccurate and impressionistic. Even within Europe itself the size and topography of individual states was often wildly imprecise. Alessandro Farnese, the commander of Philip II's armies fighting the rebellious Dutch in 1585, appears to have believed that Holland was an island; and when the first truly accurate survey was made of the kingdom of France, Louis XIV complained that his cartographers had robbed him of several hundred square miles of territory.

Yet, if the limits of Europe itself were unclear, those of Africa, Asia and America were frequently only mythical. For most ancient geographers the globe had contained a single landmass divided into three linked continents: Europe, Asia and Africa. Herodotus grumbled that he could not see 'why three names, and women's names at that, should have been given to a tract

57

which is in reality one'.) Later, Asia was divided into three: China, Japan and what were generally called 'the Indies', the lands east of the Indus, the traditional limit of the Hellenistic world. The whole of this landmass was believed to be encircled by a massive river consisting roughly of what we know as the Atlantic and Pacific Oceans. It was called by the Greeks *Okeanos*, and by later Europeans the Ocean Sea.

In the early fifteenth century, however, this vision of the world began to change. In 1434 a small fleet of lateen-rigged vessels known as caravels, barely more than fishing boats, slipped out of the Tagus estuary bound for the unknown waters of West Africa. It successfully passed Cape Bojador which jutted far out into the Atlantic from the Western Sahara and was believed by many to mark the limit of the navigable ocean. The fleet made landfall just south of the cape and then turned for home. The expedition achieved little else but it had demonstrated that it was possible to sail down the west coast of Africa and, more importantly, to return.

The early Portuguese voyages to Africa were sponsored by Prince Henry, called 'the Navigator' by later generations of admiring English sailors. In the early fifteenth century Portugal was one of the poorest nations in Europe. Denied access to the reserves of silver and gold it required, and with severely limited trading capacities, its only hope of improving its condition was to exploit its long Atlantic coastline and considerable maritime experience. Henry hoped to find a direct route to the gold which was mined somewhere in the interior of Africa and then transported overland across the Sahara by Arab middlemen to Europe. He also hoped to discover new grounds for his crusading ambitions, which had been largely frustrated on the shores of North

Africa some years before, and to make contact with the legendary Prester John. This fantastical Christian ruler of an empire of vast wealth (a confused memory of the Coptic kingdom of Ethiopia) would, so Henry hoped, make common cause with the Portuguese against the forces of Islam and help them to regain the kingdom of Jerusalem. Prince Henry found none of the things he had hoped for. The gold stayed shut up in the interior of Africa. Prester John remained confined to the realms of myth. The only crusading ventures, shameful struggles between mounted Portuguese knights and unarmed fishermen on the coasts of Mauritania, rapidly came to an end when the Portuguese moved south and the peoples of Senegal and Senegambia turned poisoned arrows upon their assailants and tsetse flies destroyed their horses. In 1448 Henry forbade any further attempt at armed conflict except in self-defence. It is often forgotten that in the first encounter between a European colonizing power and an African people the Europeans were soundly defeated.[1]

Later voyages, however, aimed at securing direct access to the silks, spices, precious woods and other luxury commodities of the East and, with more enduring and sinister consequences, to opening up the trade in African slaves. Henry died in 1460. But his initiative changed the economies of Europe, the relations of Europeans with the peoples of the world beyond, and the nature of European imperial ambitions. At first the voyages had been modest. Even in 1497, by which time the Portuguese had established a secure base in West Africa, the fleet with which on 22 November Vasco da Gama rounded the Cape of Good Hope and sailed into the Indian Ocean consisted of only four small ships. They carried a startlingly inappropriate collection of trading goods: hawks' bells, brass chamberpots, and the brass bracelets which later became the currency of the African slave trade. It was a tawdry collection of junk with which to do business with the highly sophisticated merchants of the fabled Orient. When da Gama returned to Lisbon in April 1499 and laid out before King Manuel II the precious goods he had brought back with him, the king is said to have thought for a while and then remarked that 'it would seem that it is not we who have discovered them, but they who have discovered us.'

Despite these beginnings, by the seventeenth century the Portuguese empire reached all the way from West Africa to India and southern China, and the overladen carracks of the *Carrera da India* annually carried immense fortunes back to Europe.[2] Some idea of the profits to be made from the trade in spices and silks with Asia can be had from the voyage led by Fernão de Magalhães (known to the English as Magellan), a Portuguese in the service of the Spanish crown, to find a route south to the so-called Spice Islands (the Moluccas). Magellan set sail from Sanlúcar de Barrameda on 20 September 1519 with five ships. The voyage, which led to the first circumnavigation of the globe, lasted for three years. One by one the ships foundered or sank and Magellan himself died in a skirmish on Mactan Island in the Philippines. In the end only one vessel, the *Victoria*, remained. On 8 September 1522 she sailed into Seville, leaking and with only seventeen Europeans and four Indians on board. But the spices she carried in her holds were enough to cover the costs of the entire voyage, with the loss of four ships, and still make a profit.

The Portuguese navigators had sailed into waters which many had believed to be unnavigable. They had travelled down the coast of Africa, rounded the Cape of Good Hope and reached India. More importantly, they had done all this and returned. The impact they have had on the subsequent history of the world has been enormous. But their voyage was neither so dramatic nor, arguably, so far-reaching as that undertaken in 1492 by an obscure but insistent Genoese who was convinced that the world was roughly half the size it was and that what were known as the Lands of the Great Khan – China and South-East Asia – could therefore be reached by sailing west. When on 12 October 1492 Columbus landed on a still unidentified island in the Caribbean which its inhabitants called Guarahani, he changed the European perception of the planet for ever. He did so, however, entirely unintentionally and against his own judgement. He insisted until his dying day that what he had encountered out there in the Atlantic was not a new world but merely the easternmost rim of Asia. He was not at all interested in new worlds. In his geographical understanding, the vast Ocean Sea was dotted with islands of no great wealth or significance. What Columbus had promised his sponsors, Ferdinand and Isabel, the monarchs of the united kingdoms of Castile and Aragon, was direct access by sea to the wealth of the Orient. The last thing they wanted was an unknown land peopled by naked 'savages' who had no spices or silks to offer and precious little gold or silver.

By the time Columbus returned from his third voyage in 1498, however, it had become obvious to all in Europe that America was no mere island but a continent which had been wholly unknown to antiquity (although maps were still being produced in the 1510s which eliminated the Pacific and declared Cuba to be a part of Asia). Columbus himself remained a stubbornly medieval figure who preferred to believe that the vast quantities of fresh water flowing from the Orinoco into the Gulf of Paria in modern Venezuela came from the earthly paradise rather than any new world. He was buried in Franciscan habit and left what little money remained to him at his death to sponsor a crusade.[3] But for later generations he became, like Galileo, with whom he was often compared, a hero of the new science who in defiance of the wisdom of the day had shattered all conceptions of what was known about the globe and, more importantly, what could be known. Here was a man who had demonstrated that the moderns could indeed surpass the wisdom of the ancients. Little wonder that for later generations the 'discovery' of America, along with Vasco da Gama's voyage around the Cape of Good Hope to India, came to be seen as the beginnings of the modern world.

The discovery of the existence of America, a hitherto unknown landmass of immense size and complexity, not only upset all previous notions of geography but led many to wonder if other undiscovered continents might lie to the south in the fabled Antipodes. According to St Augustine, it was absurd to suppose that men might live there because they would have to do so hanging upside down. Augustine had not supposed that the world was flat – almost no one did that. But neither had he fully grasped the significance of the sphericity of the earth. By the early sixteenth century, however, all Europeans had come to suppose that, excluding some of the deserts and the furthermost northern reaches (which were recognized as being too cold for habitation by most humans), all the world was at least potentially inhabitable. A new continent called by the cartographers 'the unknown southern land' – *Terra australis incognita* – was projected into the South Pacific. When in 1642 the Dutchman Abel Tasman landed on what is now Tasmania and the south island of New Zealand, the possibility that there existed inhabitable land in that shadowy region became a certainty – although it would take more than another century, until Captain Cook's second voyage of 1772–5, before anyone was to realize the full extent of what in 1817 was baptized by Governor Macquarie as Australia.

Charles V and his heirs, Philips II, III and IV, laid claim to all of this even though they had very little notion of what it contained. When Columbus returned in 1493 the Spanish crown immediately petitioned the papacy for title to what he had 'discovered'. This was not an unusual move. Not only did the papacy at this time act as an arbiter in international disputes, it was believed by some (although by no means all) to exercise by divine decree authority over the lands not just of Christian but also of non-Christian rulers. In 1455 Pope Nicolas V had licensed King Afonso V of Portugal to 'reduce to perpetual slavery' all the inhabitants of Africa, 'and all southern coasts until their end', as the 'enemies of Christ'. And Castile was not to be outdone. In 1493 Pope Alexander VI duly issued a series of decrees (known as bulls) which gave Ferdinand and Isabella control over all those lands 'you have discovered or are about to discover'. The peoples who inhabited these places, although the pope insisted that they should be well treated and led as gently as possible into the Christian fold, had no identity but a negative one. They were not Christians and had not yet fallen under the authority of a Christian ruler. The pope, as the American lawyer James Otis observed in 1764 with the withering sarcasm of a devout Calvinist, had thus with a single flourish of his pen 'granted away the kingdoms of the earth with as little ceremony as a man would leave a sheepcote'.

A year later, still under the watchful eye of the papacy, Spain and Portugal signed a treaty in the Spanish town of Tordesillas which for the first (and the last) time in human history divided the entire world into two areas of jurisdiction. The Tordesillas Line, as it came to be called, was drawn along longitude 46° 30′ W, calculated at 370 leagues west of the Cape Verde Islands. (Before the invention of stable marine chronometers in the seventeenth century, lines of longitude were only ever approximate, and in the eighteenth century this led to bitter border disputes between Spain and Portugal in South America.) The western half went to Castile which believed that it now controlled an unhindered route to the Orient. The eastern half went to Portugal, intent mainly on keeping its Castilian rivals out of the South Atlantic, which thereby came into possession of Brazil. But the agreement failed to say anything about what happened where East met West on the far side of the world, or who would be entitled to what portions of the fabled southern continent should one prove to exist. The treaty and the Alexandrine bulls were regarded with predictable contempt by the other European powers. Yet, despite their obvious flimsiness as documents in international law, the Spanish crown continued to insist on what one British official in 1749 described as 'their whimsical notion of exclusive right in those seas' until the final demise of the empire at the end of the eighteenth century.

In 1494 neither the Spanish nor the Portuguese had any but the vaguest of notions of what the vast tracts of ocean to which they had laid claim might contain. By the time Ferdinand's grandson, the future Charles V, set out to claim his inheritance, however, it was becoming obvious that the Indies were more than a cluster of islands inhabited by simple Stone Age cultures. The fantasy of lands filled with gold which the Portuguese had pursued along the shores of Africa, and which was to cost Sir Walter Raleigh his head, was now being relocated to America. With the conquest of Mexico in the 1520s and that of Peru a decade later, the fantasy was suddenly and dramatically transformed into reality. On this occasion, wryly commented the eighteenth-century philosopher and economist Adam Smith, Fortune had done what Fortune rarely ever does and 'favoured its devotees' with 'something not very unlike that profusion of precious metals which they sought for'. From the 1530s, when the massively rich silver mines of Mexico and Peru were discovered, until well into the eighteenth century, American silver poured unceasingly eastwards, first into the coffers of the Spanish crown and then outwards through German, Dutch and Italian bankers until it reached every part of the continent.

The 'discovery' of America meant more, however, than access to huge deposits of precious metals. The voyages of Columbus and Vasco da Gama were, said Adam Smith, 'the most important events recorded in the history of mankind', not because they had provided Europe with gold and silver, but because they had made her peoples vastly more mobile than they had ever been before.[4] They had brought them closer to the great civilizations of the Indian Ocean and into ultimately tragic contact with entire races of whose very existence they had previously known nothing. By the time Smith published *The Wealth of Nations* in 1776 the two Iberian empires had truly encompassed the globe. They had come closer to creating a single world economy than ever before. They had distributed populations across the continents and circulated new diseases, new foodstuffs, and new drugs all the way from Seville to Manila. And all of this they had done by exploiting the waters and winds of the world.

The Europeans were, of course, not alone in their use of the sea. The Arabs had extensive seaborne trading networks in the waters around the Arabian peninsula. Long before the Europeans reached them, the Polynesians had crossed vast expanses of ocean, sailing their double-hulled canoes against the wind, to colonize areas thousands of miles from their homelands, and had drawn maps to prove it – maps which astonished Captain Cook when he was shown them. Between 1405 and 1433 a Chinese admiral, Zheng He, had made seven voyages in giant, 400-foot-long, nine-masted junks called *bao chuan* or 'treasure ships', through the China Seas and the Indian Ocean from Taiwan to the Persian Gulf and down the east coast of Africa as far as Malindi and Mombassa. Zheng's mission was trade and most of his ships were laden with merchandise. But the fleet was also accompanied by supply ships, water tankers, transport for horses, warships and numerous lighter boats, with crews amounting to more than 28,000 sailors and soldiers. It was a small population under sail, the largest fleet the world had then seen, dwarfing the 100-foot vessels with which Vasco da Gama entered the same waters over half a century later.

But the Arab traders confined themselves largely to their own coastal waters, and the Polynesians never left the Pacific. After Zheng's last voyage the Chinese decided to cease all long-distance overseas trade. Why they did so no one really knows. In 1477, when a later attempt was made to revive overseas trading, the vice-president of the Ministry of War, Liu Daxia, confiscated

Zheng He's documents from the archives and either hid or burned them. They were, he said, 'deceitful exaggerations of bizarre things, far removed from the testimony of people's eyes and ears' and all that the ships had brought home had been 'betel, bamboo staves, grape wine, pomegranates, ostrich eggs and such like odd things'. China had turned its back upon any further expansion of the empire, on overseas trade and, so far as was possible, on any further contact with outsiders. It was a decision which, in the longer run, was to prove calamitous. By the mid-seventeenth century the Europeans had effective mastery of the Atlantic and were the most powerful trading presence in the Indian Ocean. By the end of the eighteenth century they had taken over most of the Pacific. When at last in 1860 the war junks of the Dragon Throne, technically unchanged since the days of Zheng, confronted the iron-clad, steam-driven gunboats of the British intruders the entire fleet was reduced to matchwood. All the English suffered was the death of one sailor, struck by a stray cannonball.

Navigation changed dramatically the future relationships between the peoples of the world. It not only brought Europeans into ever closer contact with increasingly larger areas of the globe but allowed them to transport large numbers of individuals from one part of the planet to another. Migrations, which before the creation of ocean-going sailing ships had been predominantly overland and slow and irreversible, became rapid and potentially reversible. True, the colonies of the ancient world had also depended upon the ship; and Viking seafarers had reached as far as the shores of North America, and some seem to have returned to tell the tale. But these journeys had all been dependent upon tiny, oared vessels capable of covering relatively small stretches of water. The great flotillas which would cross and recross the Atlantic and the Pacific became in the space of a very few years capable of carrying the equivalent of an entire population.

When in 1519 Charles set out for his coronation as the official heir of Augustus, he was already in name at least master of a vast new continent, and his apologists and historians were busy making good his claim in the name of the universality of the Roman *imperium* to be lord of the still vaster regions that lay beyond. Without the ship none of this would have been imaginable. Charles had had his emblem put on a sail and it was the sail which would carry it to the ends, or at least very nearly the ends, of the earth. As a result, his empire was to be the first in human history on which, in Ariosto's words, 'the sun never set'.

5 Spreading the word

The empire of Charles V was not only Roman, it was also Holy. Throughout his life Charles saw himself as the defender of Christendom against all its enemies, both external and internal. And his heirs, down to the final disintegration of the Spanish empire at the end of the eighteenth century, would remain loyal to this image. In this, too, Charles was conscious of his place as the successor to Augustus and Constantine, for Roman imperialism had also marched under the banner of religious devotion. This was focused on the emperor's own person; and all the pagan emperors had themselves deified so that their *imperium* became not merely a mundane right to rule, as it had been for the senate, but a quasi-mystic power reserved to them alone. Aurelian, in the third century AD, in emulation of Alexander, brought back to Rome the Persian worship of the unconquered sun; and his successor Diocletian came to regard himself as Jovius, the earthly representation of Jupiter. After Constantine's conversion to Christianity the practice ceased, but all Roman emperors and most Christian monarchs after them believed that the authority they possessed had been granted to them by God – until the French Revolution swept the whole notion of the divinity of kings away for ever.

For the Romans, the divinity of the emperor was indissolubly linked to the grandeur of the homeland, the *patria*, and love of the *patria* had always been an expression of individual piety among the Roman people. The Latin word *pietas*, however, meant something rather different to a pagan Roman than its modern, Christianized counterpart does. Piety, like virtue, described qualities associated ultimately with warfare: devotion, loyalty and trust, adherence to the laws of the community, and the willingness to sacrifice one's life for the common good. The truly pious man was inevitably also a warrior. 'A man outstanding in arms and piety' is how the poet Virgil introduces Aeneas, the founder of Rome, in the *Aeneid*. It was this piety which in the view of St Augustine had led God to entrust the Romans with the task of uniting the world prior to the coming of Christ. Universal empire had been their reward, he believed, for 'the virtues by which they pursued the hard road which brought them at last to such glory ... They disregarded private wealth for the sake of the common wealth. They stood firm against avarice, gave advice to their country with an unshakeable mind and were not guilty of any crime against the laws, nor of any unlawful desire.'[1]

It is not a very convincing account of the historical Roman empire, but it captures the ambiguities which followed the attempt to turn Roman martial virtues into the rather more gentle Christian ones. Piety became submissiveness before God. Virtue, which for the Romans had meant only the qualities of manliness, came to be associated with an ethic of renunciation.

Under its Christian rulers Rome would become the place where the universalizing message of Christ would find its ultimate if also unintended political expression. Christ himself might have wished the things of Caesar to remain Caesar's and, more importantly, those of God to remain for ever and only God's. But under Peter's successors in the see of Rome the borders between church and state, although hotly contested, became increasingly blurred. After Constantine's conversion Christianity, which had begun by turning its back upon empire, became and in the West was to remain empire's most valuable ally. The divinity which hedged the pagan emperors was transferred to the Christian. 'The emperor,' wrote the second-century theologian Tertullian, father of the church and scourge of deviants of any kind, 'is established in dignity by God, and [the Christian] must honour him and wish for his preservation.' Now that they could no longer claim to be divinities in their own right, the Christian Roman emperors took upon themselves the role of defenders of the church. Even after the disappearance of the empire and the rise of the new nation-states the kings of Europe acquired semi-sacred titles: 'Most Christian king' was bestowed upon Francis I of France, 'Most Catholic Monarchs' on Ferdinand and Isabella of Spain, and 'Defender of the Faith', somewhat ironically in the light of subsequent developments, on Henry VIII of England.

Christianity was also a truly universalizing creed. The 'new man', St Paul informed the Colossians, 'is being renewed unto knowledge after the image of him that created him, where there cannot be Greek or Jew, circumcision and uncircumcision, barbarian, Scythian, bondman, freeman: but Christ is all and in all'.[2] This new Christian world order, the origins of which could not now be separated from those of the Roman empire, would, as Tertullian had also said, endure as long as 'this earthly world'. It thus came to imagine itself not only as the common *patria* of humankind, but as a spiritual, cultural and moral order with no natural frontiers. From this the Christian Roman emperors took upon themselves a duty not only to uphold and protect Christendom, but also to extend the knowledge of Christ to those non-Christians who because of their ignorance had been denied historical access to the 'congregation of the faithful'.

Thenceforth, Christianity accompanied the expanding European empires almost until their final demise in the middle of the twentieth century. Where the conquerors and the settlers and traders went the missionaries followed hard behind. Priests and friars travelled on all the Portuguese voyages and accompanied all the conquering Spanish armies. For a brief period in the early sixteenth century the Spanish Caribbean was even administered by the Hieronymite order. Calvinist ministers travelled into Dutch Asia and Africa. French Huguenot pastors occupied a short-lived settlement in Brazil in the sixteenth century where one of them, Jean de Lery, wrote one of the earliest and most sympathetic accounts of a 'primitive' people ever written by a European.[3] Anglican clergymen, and even a few women, followed the flag into India and then into Uganda and Nyasaland and what became Rhodesia. Some of them did so in order to provide legitimacy to barely legitimate enterprises. Many, however, went in the hope that the journey on which they had embarked would be a stage in the final triumph of Christ over the whole world. In the Americas the fact that Hernán Cortés' conquest of Mexico had roughly coincided with Luther's rebellion was taken as a sign that God had given to the church territories in the new hemisphere to compensate for those it had lost in the old. Such millenarianism is possibly a feature of all early empires. It provided an ideology and a goal but it also offered a prediction, a certainty which could help to uplift those who felt, as many did, that sometimes things were not going quite as they had expected.

In its transition from world-renouncing sect to state religion, Christianity had become something none of its founders could ever have imagined, or wanted. The Christian church, unlike Islam, is based on layer upon layer of highly sophisticated – not to say sophistical – interpretation of its founders' words, filtered through Greek philosophy and Roman jurisprudence. In the process those words have become obscured, darkened, sometimes wilfully distorted. As a consequence the Church militant has, at least since the Middle Ages, been the constant companion of the Church pastoral. Yet Christianity itself has not always been the entirely pliant handmaiden of empire. Christ's message, with its insistence on the priority of the spiritual over the temporal, was there to be read by those who could do so. The religious orders in particular were inclined, to the displeasure not only of their secular overlords but sometimes also of their own superiors, to insist that it should be taken seriously and literally – that 'love thy neighbour as thyself' should be a real deterrent against pillage and the unwarranted expropriation of the goods of others, even when, as was generally the case, those others were not Christians.

Most of the missionaries lived in an uneasy alliance with the soldiers, adventurers, merchants, royal officials and lawyers who made up the advance forces of most colonizing voyages. The friar who protested to that archetypal conquistador Francisco Pizarro that he was not doing enough to convert the Incas to Christianity before slaughtering them received the tart reply: 'I have not come for that. I have come to take their gold away from them.' He was not alone. Jesuit and Dominican missionaries, Anglican chaplains and Huguenot pastors similarly protested against the excesses of the settlers from Brazil to

Timor. Most of them went unheard. But by no means all. One who started a debate over the rights of conquerors which was to echo down the centuries was an otherwise obscure Spanish Dominican named Antonio de Montesinos.

On the Sunday before Christmas 1511, the small and motley Spanish population of the island of Hispaniola filed into the main church of the town, then barely more than a village, of Santo Domingo. It was hot and humid and the church was a small rudimentary structure of adobe bricks under an agave roof. Diego Colón, Columbus' brother and the governor of the island, was there with all the other king's men. Most of those who made up the congregation were 'holders' (encomenderos) of Indians, as they were called. Encomenderos were entitled to exploit the labour of the Indians, although not to take their lands, and in exchange they were supposed to look after their spiritual welfare and even to pay them a small wage. Most, however, did none of this. They had crossed the ocean in the belief that they could become in this new world what they could never have been in the old, and they resented the crown's refusal to allow them simply to enslave the Indians and appropriate their lands. That morning, they had all come to the church because they had been told that the sermon would contain a special message for them. One of them, who left an impassioned and detailed account of all that followed, was a lay-priest called Bartolomé de Las Casas. When Las Casas entered the church that day he was a holder of Indians like all the rest, a little kinder perhaps than most but largely untroubled by the misery he saw about him. He would leave a changed man, the man who would become the 'Defender and Apostle to the Indians', the perpetual moral scourge of the Spanish settler community and a hero for anticolonialists from that day to this.

The dignitaries of the island had also come to hear Montesinos because he was known as a 'great lover of the rigours of religion', a very devout and fiery preacher, 'very chloeric in his words'. The sermon they got was certainly choleric. But it was no ordinary exhortation of the kind to which they were accustomed. Montesinos mounted the crude wooden pulpit. Having begun with a few obvious and unthreatening things about Advent, he launched 'with pugnacious and terrible words' into an attack on the conscience of the Spaniards which he likened to a 'sterile desert'. They were words, Las Casas later remembered, which 'made the Spaniards' flesh creep as if they already stood before divine judgement'. Montesinos thundered at them, demanding to know by what right they treated 'these innocent people', the Indians, 'with such cruelty and tyranny', by what authority they had 'made such detestable wars against peoples who were living pacifically and gently on their own lands'. Montesinos' ringing questions culminated in three which were to become the rallying cry of the struggle against colonial rulers in the Spanish-speaking world and far beyond. 'Are these not men?' he asked. 'Do they not have rational souls? Are you not obliged to love them as yourselves?'[4]

Las Casas listened appalled. From that moment, which he thought of as his 'conversion', right until the end of his very long life (he lived to be ninety-two years old), he dedicated himself to a single objective: that of demonstrating first to his king, then to the royal administration – the Council of the Indies – and finally to the world at large that the American Indians were human beings and had a right to be treated as what they were in law, true subjects of the Castilian crown. Las Casas wrote a great deal: histories, political and theological treatises, ethnographies, and innumerable pamphlets. He also did a great deal. In 1543 he was made bishop of Chiapus in southern Mexico, a region which from his day to this has been a predominantly Indian area and has always refused to accept quietly the rule of usurpers, be they Spanish conquistadors or modern Mexican *politicos*. Twice between 1545 and 1560, once in Cumaná on the Venezuelan coast and then in the optimistically named Verapaz ('True Peace') in what is now Honduras, he attempted to establish communities of the kind the missionaries believed they might have been able to create if the Spanish colonists had not got there first: settlements of priests and honest farmers. Both projects, however, turned out to be based upon a tragic illusion. No one leaves his home for an uncertain life in remote lands except in the hope of being able to better himself. The 'honest farmers' recruited for Las Casas' experiments had a rather more conventional view of what improvement meant than he did. Even before they had reached America they were boasting of how they would be wearing swords in the new world and that they had gone there to command not to obey.

Las Casas' main objectives were intellectual. He was an agitator, a rhetorician, and a pamphleteer. He fought the royal administration unremittingly, until finally in 1542 he persuaded the crown to introduce a body of legislation, the New Laws, which attempted to curb the worst excesses of the settlers and to return to the Indians at least some of their rights. These proved to be unworkable, almost provoked a settler revolt and were repealed a few years later, but they did demonstrate that rulers could be swayed by the sheer force of moral and religious indignation. Today Las Casas is probably best remembered for two things. The first is a brief and gory chronicle of all the horrors perpetrated against the Indians from the occupation of Hispaniola to Pizarro's conquest of the Inca kingdom of Peru, called succinctly *A Short Account of the Destruction of the Indies*.[5] This became a bestseller in a number of European languages. It was the book which launched the 'Black Legend' against Spain, the often distorted record of Spanish atrocities which was to darken every attempt to exonerate or even to describe Spanish imperial ventures from the sixteenth to the eighteenth centuries. The second was his role in a debate with a humanist historian and translator of Aristotle named Juan Ginés de Sepúlveda, on the rationality of the American Indians.[6]

In 1544 Sepúlveda had written a dialogue in Latin justifying the 'wars' waged against the Indians by the Spaniards. A large part of his argument hinged on the image of the Indians as subhuman creatures, filthy, ignorant, 'like pigs with their eyes fixed always on the ground', lascivious and idolatrous, given to unnatural practices such as incest, cannibalism and human sacrifice. 'Homunculi', he called them, in whom 'hardly a vestige of humanity remains'. Sepúlveda's work circulated widely in manuscript and unsurprisingly met with the approval of the settler community in Mexico which sent its author a gift of 200 pesos' worth of jewels and clothing, no small sum, to 'encourage him in the future'. When, as part of the complex business of sixteenth-century censorship, the work was submitted to the theology faculty of the University of Salamanca for approval, the theologians turned it down on the grounds that its doctrines were not 'sound' and that it was likely to cause a 'scandal'. Sepúlveda was furious. He was the official royal historian and one of the king's chaplains. He had produced a ringing defence of imperial policy and practice. To reject him in this humiliating fashion was little short of treason. Behind the decisions of the university professors he thought he saw, probably correctly, the intrigues of Las Casas. In 1549 he wrote to the future Philip II, then regent of Castile, demanding a public hearing, a debate in which his views could be made public before the Council of the Indies. This would surely vindicate all he had said.

Sepúlveda got what he had asked for. The 'debate' – although the two men seem never to have met face to face – was staged in Valladolid in 1550–51, in the presence of a number of judges appointed by both sides. Las Casas spoke for five days without ceasing from a text which he had written with 'so much sweat and sleepless nights'. He challenged not only what Sepúlveda had said but all that had ever been written against the Indians until he was asked by the Dominican Domingo de Soto, who was presiding over the whole affair, to limit himself to the arguments he was trying to refute. Some days later Sepúlveda replied to this tirade with twelve objections, to which Las Casas in turn replied with twelve replies. And so it might have gone on if Soto had not put an end to a debate which, as he said, had 'now grown as long and prolix as the years of this matter'.

The outcome was inconclusive. One of judges, Melchor Cano, left before the end and was still being asked for his judgement seven years later; and Soto himself, although he was generally unsympathetic to most forms of empire, abstained. Sepúlveda's little book was not published until the nineteenth century so in some sense Las Casas and the theologians of Salamanca could be said to have won. This is certainly how the whole event was later understood. When in 1763 Boswell asked Doctor Johnson what he thought of the Spanish empire, Johnson replied, 'I love the university of Salamanca, for when the Spaniards were in doubt as to the lawfulness of their conquering America, the university of Salamanca gave it as their opinion that it was not lawful.'[7]

Johnson had not got it quite right. But for him and for many of those who, as he did, cordially detested most forms of colonialism, the debate had become symbolic of the power of moral outrage to halt, or at least slow down, the process of empire. It has been seen, too, as evidence of the other side of European imperialism, the self-scrutinizing, even self-hating fear that in the end all this might have done far greater damage than it had ever done good – far greater damage, furthermore, not only to the benighted peoples of the worlds beyond Europe but also to the Europeans themselves. Las Casas had expressed this in eschatological, apocalyptic, prophetic terms, warning Spaniards that if they did not soon mend their ways God would destroy them as he had done once before, by sending the Muslims to conquer them in 711. Later writers, such as the French philosopher Montesquieu, reflecting on the Spanish case in the eighteenth century, and the liberal political theorist Alexis de Tocqueville, commenting on French Algeria in the nineteenth, would warn other generations of unrepentant imperialists that no one can afford for long to practise atrocities and tyrannies overseas without the evil that they do seeping back to contaminate the homeland.

To later generations Las Casas became a symbol of the fight

against the injustices of colonialism. In 1810, Simón Bolívar, 'The Liberator' of South America, described him as, 'that friend of humanity who with such fervour and determination denounced to his government and his contemporaries the most horrific acts of that sanguineous frenzy'. Even in Spain itself, despite murmurings of protest from the Catholic reactionaries of the late nineteenth century, he has been hailed as the 'authentic expression of the true Spanish conscience', in an attempt to explain away the destruction of the Amerindian peoples as a passing aberration in the nation's history. For many, in Spain and beyond, his presence has seemed somehow to redeem the inescapable complicity of all Europe in the Spanish conquests. The Abbé Guillaume Raynal, author together with the philosopher and man-of-letters Denis Diderot, of the *Philosophical and Political History of the Two Indies* of 1780, the fiercest and most widely read condemnation of European colonialism written during the Enlightenment, looked forward to a more generous age when 'these unfortunate lands which have been destroyed will be repopulated and acquire laws, customs, justice and liberty'. He imagined a statue, 'In which you will be shown standing between the American and the Spaniard, holding out your breast to the dagger of the latter to save the life of the former. And on the base such words as these should be inscribed: IN A CENTURY OF FEROCITY, LAS CASAS, WHO YOU SEE BEFORE YOU, WAS A BENEVOLENT MAN.'[8] Today, throughout the Americas there are many such statues. In Latin America Las Casas' presence remains a powerful one. He has been represented as a kind of Catholic Marxist *avant la lettre* and is looked upon as the founding father of liberation theology, the semi-heterodox movement within the Latin American church which has tried to direct the attention of the clergy once again to the suffering of the poor and the oppressed.

But for all the passion of his rhetoric, Las Casas was no modern critic of colonialism. He was firmly committed to the view that the Americas were the legitimate property of the crown of Spain. He even went so far as to say so in his will. He never doubted the superiority of European civilization, never doubted that without Christ the inhabitants of the Americas would have been doomed to eternal damnation, never doubted that it was only with the coming of Columbus that 'these numberless peoples who had laid in oblivion throughout so many centuries' had finally entered history. Las Casas' reading of history both legitimated the Spanish occupation of the Americas in the name of the church and ultimately made the Europeans the paternal instructors of all those who would later come to be called the 'backward' races of the world. What it did not do was to sanction the indiscriminate exploitation of these races, nor did it deprive them of their humanity or their rights. As Las Casas insisted time and again, although God's deliverance of the Americas to the Castilian crown had granted it incontestable political rights, it had imposed upon it a severe moral duty which, at least during his lifetime, it had done very little to fulfil.

6   The decline of the Iberian world

Las Casas' protests against the cruelty of the Spanish settlers had been made not only when Spain was the most powerful state in Europe but when its ruler, Charles V, could reasonably claim to be the heir to Augustus, the bringer of order and peace to the entire world. In 1555–6, exhausted by his struggles to keep his scattered domains together and to contain the menace of Protestantism, Charles abdicated in favour of his son Philip and retired to the remote Spanish monastery of Juste. There he spent the remainder of his days eating gargantuan meals and playing with ingenious clockwork toys. In the complex process of succession Philip lost the Austrian homelands, Germany and Bohemia, together with the imperial title, to his uncle Ferdinand. But in 1580 he acquired through the uncertainties of dynastic succession the kingdom of Portugal and with it the now sprawling Portuguese overseas empire. This vast conglomerate, the Catholic Monarchy as it came to be known, lasted until 1640 and it spanned the entire globe.

Only parts of Asia, China and India now lay seemingly beyond Philip's reach. In 1565, Spanish forces seized what were called in his honour the Philippines, and there, close to the Asian mainland, fantastical plots began to be hatched for the invasion of China. In 1584, the bishop of Malacca, João Ribeiro Gaio, came up with a scheme for a joint Spanish and Portuguese attack on the Chinese mainland by way of Sumatra, Patani and Thailand. Two years later a 'general assembly of the Spanish inhabitants of the Philippines' led by the bishop and the governor drew up a petition urging the king to prepare for the conquest of China and entrusted a Jesuit, Alonso Sánchez, to carry it in person to the king. Nothing came of this. The great Italian Jesuit sinologist Matteo Ricci, who had adopted Chinese dress and been accepted into the Chinese intelligentsia, poured scorn on the project. He knew that China was endless and alien, that no European monarch, however great, could sustain the allegiance of such distant and complex peoples, that his armies would lose themselves in the inner wastes of the empire and starve to death.[1] Neither was Philip himself, despite his occasional messianic claims to universal empire, able to contemplate any further expansion. For all his conviction that he was doing God's work in the world, he was not a Holy Roman emperor and most of his efforts and most of his wealth went not into conquering and converting all that remained of the world but into sustaining what he had inherited, a monarchy which slowly but inexorably was beginning to unravel.

What contemporaries called 'the decline of Spain' had, however, already begun by the mid-sixteenth century.[2] In 1568 the Netherlands, the heart of the old Duchy of Burgundy where Charles V had been born, rose in revolt. A long and bitter war ensued which gradually drew in most of the states of Europe, squandered massive resources and millions of lives and, in its final stages, spread across half the globe. It lasted, on and off, for eighty years until in 1648 the Spanish were finally driven to acknowledge the existence of the new state. Already in 1579 the United Netherlands (modern Holland) as it was known, had become first in practice and then in law a republic. For the first time in European history, a rebellious vassal state had succeeded in acquiring self-determination. The new republic now stood poised to become an imperial power in its own right.

Spain was financially and morally bankrupted by what the Dutch call the Eighty Years War (and the Spanish the Revolt of the Netherlands). Burdened with the need to hold together diverse, over-extended states, Philip II and his successors Philip III and IV had been overly concerned with the short-term gains of war and insufficiently mindful of the long-term economic needs of the various peoples of which their monarchy was composed. Spain, and Castile in particular, had been hit by the runaway inflation that had followed the importation of astonishing quantities of silver and gold from America. No one at the time really understood the mechanisms of inflation or had very much idea about how economics in general worked. In a world without monetary policies, economic crises were all too often attributed to God's disfavour. Neither did anyone have any clear idea about the relationship between wealth and scarcity, and precious metals tended to be treated as fetishes rather than as means of exchange. Columbus had been so certain of the inherent power of gold that he had once declared it could make a man 'jump into heaven'. As Adam Smith pointed out later, Spain's problems could all be attributed to the failure to understand that the increase in the production of bullion could only ever lead to its devaluation. 'The same passion,' he wrote, 'which has suggested to many people the absurd idea of the philosopher's stone, has suggested to others the equally absurd one of immense rich mines of gold and silver. They did not consider that the value of those metals has, in all ages and nations, arisen chiefly from their scarcity.'³

Because of its rulers' obsession with the illusory wealth to be found in precious metals, Spain had also failed to develop the potential of its overseas possessions for trade and agriculture. Many of the more far-sighted conquistadors, Hernán Cortés among them, had been eager to stress the potentially disastrous consequences of the grab-and-run mentality that had marked the early conquests. Few wanted to see a repetition of the virtual devastation of the population of the Antilles, which followed on the Spanish conquest. Yet despite moderate reforms, the maintenance of the supply of gold and silver continued to be the crown's principal economic concern. Even in the 1770s and 1780s, when a concerted effort was made to modernize the empire according to free-trade principles, the final objective was the reinvigoration of the production of the silver mines. Time and again the Spanish crown was forced to default on its loans. The economy slid into stagnation. What resources there were went increasingly into protecting Spanish and Portuguese over-seas possessions and shipping from attack by the new con-tenders for control of the world's oceans, the English, the French and, as they broke free of their Spanish masters, the Dutch.

Even by the late sixteenth century, the Dutch had begun an onslaught on the Portuguese possessions in Asia, which were far more vulnerable than the Spanish colonies in America. By the mid-seventeenth century they had taken Cochin, Malacca, Sumatra, Java, Borneo, the Celebes, the Moluccas, the western end of New Guinea, Formosa and, most importantly, Indonesia. When in 1658 they finally managed to seize Ceylon all that remained of the Portuguese empire in the East Indies was Goa in southern India and Macao. Portugal held on to Brazil until 1822, despite Dutch and French incursions, and her settlements in West Africa until the mid-twentieth century, but the empire that Prince Henry had set in motion in 1434 had relinquished most of its wealth and all its power by the end of the seventeenth century.[4]

Slowly Spain also began to lose its grip on its overseas empire. By the mid-seventeenth century much of the trade between the colonies was being carried in foreign ships, largely to the benefit of foreign merchants. By the 1680s, the French had moved south from Canada to found New Orleans, French and English buccaneers had sacked Panama, Cartagena and Veracruz; and Spain's naval power had fallen so low that during the War of the Spanish Succession (1702–13) French warships were used to escort the treasure fleets home from New Spain. The war followed the death in 1700 of the last of the Habsburg kings, Charles II, known as the 'bewitched', a man who was probably impotent, certainly feeble-minded, and whose reign had been, in the words of the Venetian ambassador, 'an uninterrupted series of disasters'. When the war ended, a branch of the French Bourbon family had gained control of the Spanish throne which they have retained, with interruptions, to this day. In the process Spain lost all her remaining European possessions and the empire was reduced, in effect, to the Americas and the Philippines. These would remain, although increasingly independent and reliant upon foreign trade, for another century.

By the beginning of the nineteenth century, however, the Spanish colonists, as the English had done before them, began to resent the autocratic presence of a remote and declining European power with which few of them could now identify.

Between 1808 and 1826 in a series of bloody wars the Kingdoms of the Indies, as they had been called, were finally extinguished. In their place there arose a number of competing, mutually hostile and internally unstable republics, which have remained divided and unsettled to this day. Finally in 1898, the United States occupied and 'liberated' the Philippines, and drove the Spanish out of Cuba and Puerto Rico. The sun had now set on an empire which, at its height, had covered more than half the globe.

7 *Empires of liberty, empires of trade*

Within less than a century Europeans had taken possession of much of America and had established enduring footholds in Asia and Africa. This rapid overseas expansion had been made possible by social and economic changes in the emerging European nation-states, the development of new navigational techniques, and the evolution of ships that could sail rapidly and effectively against the wind. They had taken place, too, against the background of one of the most enduring social transformations in the history of the continent of Europe itself. On 18 April 1521, an otherwise obscure Augustinian monk named Martin Luther appeared before Charles V at the imperial diet at the city of Worms to answer charges of heterodoxy. Luther's rebellion against the Catholic church might have passed largely unperceived. There had, after all, been many protests against the corruptions of the clergy as well as theological objections, like Luther's, to the notion that the church might have some say in who gained God's favour and who did not. But the German princes and free cities chose to make use of this somewhat dyspeptic monk to mount a resistance to Charles V's increasing attempt to transform the Holy Roman empire from a loose federation of independent states into a true empire.

Their quarrel with the emperor broadened into prolonged confessional conflict. Since it was always hard to distinguish religion from politics, this rapidly developed into ideological warfare. It was the first time that the peoples of Europe had confronted one another not over dynastic claims or rights of succession, but over differences in belief. From the War of the League of Schmalkalden (an alliance of Protestant princes and cities) in 1546–7 until the Treaty of Westphalia in 1648, which finally brought to an end the Thirty Years War, one or another region of Europe was convulsed by the most bloody and ferocious civil and ideological struggle in its history prior to the outbreak of the Second World War.

The Treaty of Westphalia changed all this – or at least so it seemed to contemporaries. It was the first truly modern treaty. (Most previous ones had been little more than agreements to cease hostilities.) It created what has come to be called the Europe of Nations. It established, if only in a shadowy way, the conception of an international community and it ratified the existence of two new states, both republics: the United Netherlands and the Swiss Confederation. By the terms of the agreement, to which all the major powers of Europe were party, it would no longer be possible for nations to fight among themselves over how to interpret God's intentions for humankind. Now it would be the ruler of each state who would decide what brand of Christianity was followed in his realm. The papacy, which had acted, if often fitfully and ineffectually, as an arbiter in international disputes, would henceforth be relegated to the sidelines, its power limited to the realm of the sacred and no longer universal or very powerful even there.

By the time the treaty was signed, the map of Europe had undergone a transformation. Where once there had been religious unity across most of the continent, a confessional curtain had been lowered which separated a largely Protestant north from a largely Catholic south. This divide was not merely religious. It was also cultural, political and economic. By the middle of the seventeenth century new ideas in the arts and the sciences were moving steadily northwards. The imperial powers of the Iberian peninsula, although still among the richest in Europe, were clearly in decline. Their old enemies, France, England and the Netherlands, were in the ascendant. London and Amsterdam replaced Lisbon and Madrid. A pattern had been set which would last until the twentieth century.

In the process of transformation the old European visions of universal empire had faded away. Among other things, the Reformation had been a struggle against a new kind of imperialism in Europe. It is not surprising that the new Protestant nations which it finally created should have evolved their own notions of what empire could and should be. No one nation in Europe could aspire to dominate even a substantial part of the continent. Nor could any one claim to be entitled to conquer the world, although they might attempt to gain some other kind of control over it.

The balance had shifted in other ways, too. The lure of the Spanish empire had lain initially in the vast quantities of gold and silver it had been able to extract from the Americas. At first, the French and the English had merely set out to do the same. The French navigator Jacques Cartier embarked on his first expedition to what is now Canada in 1534, just as Columbus had before him, with the aim of 'discovering certain islands and lands where it is said that a great quantity of gold and other rich things might be discovered'. Like Columbus, he had returned with tales of a mysterious land of untold wealth.

But all he had to show for it were some samples of ore which on examination turned out to be not gold and silver but iron pyrites and quartz.[1] Similarly, the expeditions that Martin Frobisher led to Newfoundland in 1576, 1577 and 1578 had all gone in search of precious metals. They, too, had returned empty-handed. All Frobisher had been able to bring back were two 'Eskimos' from Baffin Island who, he explained, were, in the absence of anything more serviceable, 'tokens from thence of his being there'. They only lived for a year, exhibits for the amusement of the aristocracy, who watched them hunting the royal swans on the Thames from a skin-covered boat. They were nothing more than curiosities, part of the contemporary passion for exotica, the living equivalent of the unicorn horns and pickled mermaids to be found in the cabinets of curios which adorned many noblemen's homes.[2]

By the beginning of the seventeenth century it had become evident to all the new would-be imperial powers that the future lay not in the vain pursuit of further Aztec and Inca empires or the fantastical El Dorado – the elusive land of gold, the failure to find which had in 1618 cost Sir Walter Raleigh his head. It lay instead in trade, that new 'golden ball', as the Scot Andrew Fletcher of Saltoun called it in 1704, 'for which all nations of the world are contending'. And the only way to secure this golden ball was through mastery of the world's oceans. In the end even Raleigh, England's only would-be conquistador, came to see this. 'Whosoever commands the Sea,' he reflected, 'commands the trade, whosoever commands the trade of the world, commands the riches of the world and consequently the world itself.'[3]

The new discoveries made it obvious to all that domination of the lands and peoples of the world was beyond the reach of even the most powerful European nation. Control of the seas, however, clearly was not. A new form of universalism took hold. The empires of the largely Protestant and increasingly capitalist north would, like their predecessors, encircle the globe. But unlike their predecessors, they would all be, nominally at least, trading empires, largely eschewing colonization and conquest except as a means of last resort. They were to be built upon wealth, not military might. This involved what, by the mid-eighteenth century, was to become a massive shift in sensibilities. The rise in Britain and France of a new merchant class, educated, generally enlightened and with very little stake in the older military aristocracies, led to a powerful celebration of the civilizing and humanizing power of commerce. For commerce involved not merely the exchange of goods. It also demanded contact between peoples and with that, or so it was hoped, greater understanding and tolerance among them. 'Everything in the universe,' wrote the Marquis de Mirabeau in 1758, 'is commerce because by commerce one must understand all the natural and indispensable relationships of the entire species, which are, and will always be those between one man and another, between one family, one society, one nation and another.'

Many were also convinced that commerce was the only means to put an end to international conflict, for there was a widespread conviction that, in Diderot's words, 'A war among commercial nations is a fire that destroys them all.' Like the not dissimilar modern belief that democracies never go to war with one another, this proved in time to be an illusion since commerce could, and generally did, become as much a source of conflict as of peace. But the association of commerce with both peace and liberty survived even the great trade wars of the late eighteenth and early nineteenth centuries. 'War then comes before commerce,' as the French liberal Benjamin Constant expressed it in 1813, after witnessing the collapse of the Napoleonic empire; 'the former is all savage impulse, the latter civilized calculation.'[4]

Paradoxically perhaps, the earliest European overseas empire to be almost wholly concerned with trade rather than conquest was the Portuguese. As we have seen, the first Portuguese attempts at settlement and conquest in Africa had been thwarted by the skill of the Africans, the climate and disease. In the end, the Portuguese had been compelled to confine their settlements to coastal enclaves leased to them by local rulers. These, which they called *feitorias* or factories, a term which the British would later adopt, were established throughout Africa, India and Asia: on the island of San Jorge da Mina, at Arguin, Mozambique and Melindi, in Hormuz in the Persian Gulf, Goa and Cochin in India, and Malacca and Macao in China. They were self-governing, independent communities which, although fortified and garrisoned, existed with the consent and in most cases the active participation of the local populations. The propagandists of the Portuguese empire, in particular the epic poet Luís de Camões, were inclined to describe trade as a kind of conquest. They insisted in their legal wrangles with the Dutch that they had 'discovered' both Africa and India; and ever since the mid-fifteenth century Portuguese kings had styled themselves Lords of India and Lords of Guinea. In fact, though, the only true colony the Portuguese established anywhere was in Brazil.

Britain and Holland were the European powers that truly made commerce the ideological basis of far-reaching imperial claims. Each recognized its similarity to the other. (England had, after all, played an important role in securing Dutch independence from Spain.) They also accused one another of exploiting commerce to achieve the kind of world dominance which had for so long eluded the Spanish. The Dutch, declared the English poet Robert Wild in 1673, 'Though to grasp a power as great as old Rome / Striving to carry all commerce away / And make the universe their only prey'. When a Dutchman in a tavern asked why the English called him a 'butterbox', he was told it was because 'you are so apt to spread everywhere, and for your sauciness must be melted down'.[5] To which the Dutch could have replied that they had not driven the Spanish out of the Netherlands and pursued the Portuguese to Java and beyond only to find the British trying to take their place.

Trade, as both peoples understood it, was not merely a different means of pursuing similar universal objectives to the older imperial orders. It was an entirely different way of perceiving both what an empire was and what it might become. Trade represented a different way of construing the relationships between imperialists and aboriginal peoples, and a new approach to building colonial settlements. Whereas Alexander the Great, the Romans and all their would-be heirs had sought the possession of lands and the subjugation of peoples, the maritime empires had no concern for either land or subjugation. 'The Sea,' declared Andrew Fletcher in 1698, 'is the only Empire which can naturally belong to us. Conquest is not our Interest.'[6]

These seaborne empires were also built upon the conviction, which survives in one form or another to this day, that successful commerce and capital accumulation can only take place in free societies. In their own eyes, the British and the Dutch lived under free constitutional governments, unlike the priest-ridden subjects of the Catholic Monarchy. Their empires would encircle the entire globe as surely as those of their rivals, but they would avoid all the horrors – the unrestrained destruction of indigenous peoples, depopulation, and massive inflation – which had afflicted their Iberian rivals. They would bring the maximum benefit to the metropolis at the minimum cost to all those involved, Europeans and non-Europeans, colonizers and colonized alike. Their role would not be to exploit the resources of the defenceless peoples of the non-European world but to help them overcome paganism and primitive modes of production as well, of course, as the tyranny of other Europeans. The American Indians, declared the sixteenth-century historian and geographer Richard Hakluyt, were a people 'crying out to us ... to come and help'. (This sentiment was even incorporated in 1629 into the seal of the Massachusetts Bay Company, on which an Indian is depicted saying 'Come Over and Help Us'.)[7] Little wonder that when in the 1690s the Scots attempted to found a settlement on the Isthmus of Darien, 'peaceably ... without either Fraud or Force', they fully expected the Indians to welcome them as liberators from the 'hellish servitude and oppression' they had suffered at the hands of the Spanish. To Indian eyes, however, one heavily-armed white interloper was much like another and they fled, leaving the Spanish to finish with the Scots.[8]

England's great rival for empire in the Americas, and, to a lesser degree, India, however, was not Spain or Portugal but France. The French and the English engaged in a prolonged and heated territorial dispute from the very early seventeenth century. In 1609, when only a handful of settlers were clinging to the malarial swamps of the St James River, the first royal charter for the Virginia Company solemnly laid claim to all of America north of the border with what is now New Mexico and all the islands 'thereunto adjacent or within one hundred miles of the coast thereof'. The French retaliated in 1627 when they had just 107 settlers in Canada, situated in the regions of Acadia and the St Lawrence and completely isolated from one another, by asserting their rights over a territory reaching from Florida to the Arctic Circle, nearly all of which was uncharted. These disputes led to intermittent warfare between the two powers, in which the Indians skilfully played one side off against the other so as to preserve their own autonomy, a strategy which Peter Wraxall, secretary for Indian affairs in New York in the mid-eighteenth century, called 'the Modern Indian Politics'.[9]

Before the mid-eighteenth century these clashes had been sporadic and indecisive. In 1756, however, the two nations went to war as a consequence of a dispute involving the attempt by the Austrian Habsburgs to seize the Duchy of Silesia. The Seven Years War (or the French and Indian War), as it came to be called, was the first prolonged conflict between two European imperial powers which was fought extensively in their overseas territories. In 1763, by which time it had become obvious that France had nothing further to gain by continuing the struggle, the two sides signed the Treaty of Paris. This gave Britain all of North American east of the Mississippi, including Spanish Florida, as well as Senegal and French India, the capital of which, Pondichery, had been captured in 1761. The end of the Seven Years War left Britain indisputably the most powerful of the European maritime powers. It also left the crown with a crippling debt. For the next twelve years the government attempted to make up some of its financial losses by taxing the American colonists. This, and the crown's refusal to allow the colonies direct representation in parliament, precipitated the crisis which led ultimately to the American War of Independence.

In 1775, the British government prepared to fight a long and bitter war of attrition in its American colonies. It was, in the view of many, including the Irish orator and political philosopher Edmund Burke and the philosopher and economist Adam Smith, a doomed enterprise. The distance alone meant that any such struggle could only result in a British defeat, if not in the short then certainly in the long run. 'The Ocean remains,' Burke told the House of Commons on the outbreak of the war, 'you cannot pump it dry; and as long as it continues in its present bed, so long all the causes which weaken authority by distance will continue.'[10] It would be far better, suggested Adam Smith the following year, to let the American colonists go their own way in peace. They would make firmer friends and more valuable trading partners than they had ever made subjects.[11] The government of George III, of course, paid no heed since, as Smith himself sadly acknowledged, what was at stake in the war was not merely economic benefit. It was also honour. Had Britain surrendered America without a struggle, her empire would have been 'so much curtailed, [that] her power and dignity would be supposed to be proportionately diminished'. It would take a war – a civil war as it has sometimes been described – lasting eight bitter years to make her finally relinquish her hold over the colonies.

For men like Burke and Smith, the War of Independence made it obvious that the patterns of colonization that had evolved over the centuries since Columbus' first voyage had been a disaster. In the first instance, conquest and settlement created dependent communities which demanded massive and constant assistance from the metropolis if they were to survive. Later, when these had become strong (and potentially profitable), they obstinately insisted on going their own way like troublesome children grown to adulthood. Their inhabitants inevitably became new and different peoples. Edmund Burke could see this even before the English Americans had become simply Americans. 'The object,' he wrote of America, 'is wholly new in the world. It is singular ... nothing in history is parallel to it. All the reasoning about it, that are likely to be solid, must be drawn from its actual circumstances.'[12] Something similar was said by Simón Bolívar in 1810 about the peoples of his future, all-too brief state of Gran Colombia. Something like it was also voiced much later, perhaps in a more muted way, by New Zealanders, Australians and Afrikaners.

For the British, the American War and the loss of the Thirteen Colonies marked a watershed between what have come to be called the first and the second British empires. The focus of the latter would be in Asia, Africa and, later, the Pacific. It was an empire which set out to be all that the older empires had not been: commercial, benevolent, and liberal. As the British were proud of saying, even before the American revolution, Britain's empire was one of liberty. Not liberty, or at least not complete liberty, for its subject peoples, but liberty for its settler populations and, above all, liberty from the kind of crushing power which the creation of large empires so often placed in the hands of the military. Building such an empire was not, however, to be an easy task. 'There is not,' Edmund Burke had warned the House of Commons in 1766, any 'more difficult subject for the understanding of men than to govern a Large Empire upon a plan of Liberty.'

Burke, and many of the more perceptive thinkers in the troubled years of the American War of Independence, struggled hard to replace the vision of the British empire as a new Augustan Rome with Cicero's image of a 'commonwealth of all the world'. In 1775 the English radical John Cartwright came up with a plan to transform the empire into a 'Grand League of Confederacy'. This would have granted independence to all but a few of the strategic colonies – Newfoundland, Gibraltar, Minorca – and incorporated them within a kind of harmonious alliance in which, as he put it, 'this enlightened, this Christian kingdom' would go on to 'extend the influence of her religion and laws, not the limits of her empire' over the rest of the globe.[13] It was a vision rather than a proposal because, as Cartwright knew, no state, let alone a powerful centralist monarchy, has ever been known to relinquish what it has to the interests of some possible future, however attractive. But it captured an acceptable image of empire, one which in a not dissimilar form would reappear nearly two hundred years later as the Commonwealth, even if today that has become little more than a desperate attempt to preserve a vanished past.

In keeping with their image of themselves as nations of enlightened merchant adventurers rather than conquistadors, the first English and Dutch settlements in Asia were not colonies as they had been in America but factories similar to the Portuguese. The Dutch and English factories in Amboina, Surat, Madras, Calcutta and Bombay were all acquired by treaty and rapidly became international entrepôts, mixed communities of European and Asian merchants. Even if they had wanted to pursue more aggressive policies, neither power was in a position to do so. Although by 1658 the Dutch had ousted the Portuguese, neither they nor the English were any match for the forces of the Mughal empire. The brief skirmish between the East India Company and the Mughal armies in 1688–9 only resulted in the closure of the factory at Surat and the blockade of Bombay.

However, as the East India Company grew in strength so, too, did the temptation to use its power to control as well as to trade. In the early decades of the eighteenth century the Asian world had begun slowly but inexorably to change. The Muslim empires – Safavid, Ottoman and Mughal – which even at the middle of the century still nominally controlled between them all the lands from Algeria to the borders of Burma, were everywhere in retreat or decline. By 1765 the British were dominant in Bengal, the Deccan and Arcot. Gradually the East India Company became the true ruler of large areas of India although it remained until its dissolution by the crown in 1858 a vassal state, in name at least, of the Mughal emperor in Delhi.[14]

By the time Benjamin Disraeli had Queen Victoria declared 'Empress of India' in 1878, India and large areas of Africa had become in effect conquest states. Despite what might seem to be a reversion to earlier methods of conquest and settlement, British India differed in many crucial respects from British America – and from the European colonies which were to emerge in southern Africa in the nineteenth century. India, and Asia generally, was always a place of passage, not of settlement. It was governed by the British in British interests. But it was manned and at the lower levels administered largely by Indians. As the Persian chronicler Ghulam Husain Khan had noticed by the late eighteenth century, the English had 'a custom of coming for a number of years, and then of going away to pay a visit to their native land, without any one of them showing an inclination to fix himself in this land'.[15] The American colonists, by contrast, had gone with every intention of 'fixing' themselves in the land. They had gone to create in what they took to be a natural wilderness the worlds that they had lost in Europe or from which their social position had excluded them. Those who went to India did so only in order to return home richer than they had left. No sense of being a distinct people ever emerged among the Europeans in India. There was never a creole population or very much of the interracial breeding which transformed the population of many of the former Spanish-American colonies into truly multiethnic communities. The Anglo-Indians are still entitled to separate representation in the Indian parliament, but this remains a courtesy to the departed regime and reflects neither their numbers nor their political importance.

The absence of a dominant settler population and the fact that the British in India ruled through, and nominally on behalf of, the Mughal Emperor did not, however, prevent the agents of the Company from attempting to replicate all the worst excesses, real and imaginary, of the Spaniards in America. 'Turn your eyes to India,' wrote the English radical Richard Price in 1776. 'There more has been done than is now attempted in America. There Englishmen, actuated by the love of plunder and the spirit of conquest, have depopulated whole kingdoms and ruined millions of innocent peoples by the most infamous oppression and rapacity. The justice of the nation has slept over these enormities. Will the justice of heaven sleep? Are we not now execrated on both sides of the globe?'[16]

At the centre of this image was the figure of Warren Hastings, governor-general of Bengal from 1772 to 1785. Hastings had amassed a personal fortune, it was said, at the Company's expense and had extorted funds by force from the rulers of Benares and Avadh. 'There would seem,' remarked one of the judges at the trial for his impeachment in 1788, 'no species of peculation from which the Honourable Governor-General has thought it reasonable to abstain.' He had also, on his own admission, ruled Bengal as an 'Oriental despot'. Hastings was finally acquitted in 1795, but his trail was a great theatrical event in which were played out all the passions and anxieties that by the late eighteenth century had come to torment most European imperial states. It was stage-managed in large measure by Edmund Burke.

Burke was a great conservative and passionate denouncer of all modes of political passion. But he shared with such radicals as Price, whom he otherwise loathed, a hatred of any kind of behaviour he saw as tyrannical. The East India Company had, he claimed, become 'one of the most corrupt and destructive tyrannies that probably ever existed'.[17] Under Hastings' governorship it had perpetrated 'cruelties unheard-of, and devastations almost without name'. It had abused its power to further its own ends and, worse, it had trampled on those of its Indian subjects to whom, in Burke's conception of liberty, it owed a duty of benevolence every bit as great as to any of its European agents. To argue, as Hastings had done, that to win respect in Asia one had to rule as an Asian was to threaten all the principles, political and moral, on which the British constitution rested. It was to let 'barbarism' in. It was that most unforgivable of colonial crimes, to 'go native'.

Hastings' views horrified Burke for much the same reason as the presence of the Yorkshirewoman turned Indian would later horrify Borges' grandmother. For Burke knew, as did she, how delicate the tissue of 'civilization' and 'liberty' was, and how very easy it was to slip through it and then on down the human scale into the disordered worlds that lay only a very short distance below. Empire had given the Europeans enormous responsibilities towards the poor benighted 'savages'. It had hugely enhanced their sense of their superior grasp of what it was to be fully human. But it had also brought them face to face with both the realities and the temptations of barbarism. Burke and the enlightened rationalists of his day understood all human history to be a perpetual cycle in which barbarism gave way to civilization, only to be replaced once more by barbarism as civilization decayed, became weak, corrupt, and overrun by that most feared of eighteenth-century ills, 'luxury'. In 1776, at the precise moment when the British empire was first beginning to disintegrate, Edward Gibbon argued that in the enlightened century in which he lived the cycle appeared to have come to an end. The constant threat of a return to barbarism was, he believed, no more. But those like Burke who had heard of what had gone on beyond Europe knew otherwise.

What was on trial between 1788 and 1795 was therefore not only Warren Hastings, it was a way of governing, a way of conceiving of empire itself. Burke and the other mangers of Hastings' trial clearly harboured a deep and dispassionate concern for the well-being of the Indian subjects of the Company. They were quite sincere in their horror at what they had heard of its treatment of those who, after all, were not only free subjects but belonged to a civilization which, in some vaguely conceived sense, they recognized to be as ancient and once as great as their own. The trial was, unsurprisingly, never a popular one. Yet Burke pursued Hastings in the face of fierce opposition from those whom he once described in a letter as the 'white-men' – perhaps the first time a European has employed such an epithet for his own people.

Burke's dogged pursuit of Hastings was driven, however, by another more urgent concern. Like Las Casas before him, he realized that nothing could be practised with impunity in some distant outpost without it having consequences for the metropolis. What applied to Spain might equally apply to Britain. An Englishman could not, as Hastings had done, be an Asian despot in India without sooner or later becoming a despot also in England. To deny liberty and the right of freedom from cruelty and oppression to others could only come to undermine one's own right to such things. An empire was a whole and could only be governed as a whole. 'In order to prove that the Americans have no right to their liberties,' Burke had written of the American War, 'we are every day endeavouring to subvert the maxims which preserve the whole Spirit of our own.' The same was now true of the rights of the Indians. 'I am certain,' he wrote, 'that every means effectual to preserve India from oppression is a guard to preserve the British Constitution from its worst corruption.'[18] Empire was not the means to personal aggrandizement Hastings had made of it. It was a sacred trust 'given by an incomprehensible dispensation of Divine providence into our hands'. To abuse it might not call down the wrath of God on the head of King George – Burke shared none of Las Casas' faith in divine retribution – but it did threaten the collapse of what Burke thought of as 'the civilization of Europe'.[19]

Burke's warning, however, fell on deaf ears. The history of the British domination of India perhaps demonstrated that the lure of conquest and possession was inescapable. Britain, which had begun by condemning the Spanish and by insisting that theirs was to be an empire of trade governed in the name of liberty, had ended by becoming one of the most aggressive and rapacious of imperial powers. Yet the vision of empire as the expansion of civilization, as the benevolent rule of the more gifted and more able, as a duty as well as a right, survived the trial of Warren Hastings. By the early nineteenth century what Napoleon would call the 'civilizing mission' of the European powers came to be looked upon as an integral part of the culture of Europe. It was, after all, the one aspect of the Roman world which the modern imperialist could adopt with pride. Later, as we shall see, it became tinged with a racism which had been virtually absent from the ancient world, and in so doing it sowed the seeds of the end not only of the European overseas empires but of empire itself.

8 Slavery

The British concern to build an 'empire of liberty' for its subject peoples failed in the long run to suppress entirely the desire for the acquisition of territory. For much of its existence it also turned its face away from the dark stain that had spread across all European overseas empires: slavery.

All empires in history prior to the beginning of the nineteenth century have been slave-owning societies. Slaves were everywhere the silent and silenced masses, the peoples with whose labour Athenian democracy and Roman republicanism had been created. In antiquity 'the people' meant only the citizenry, and that excluded all slaves, as well as all women and children. The Greeks, wrote Herodotus, in what has subsequently become a commonplace, were the most free of peoples because they alone were subject not to the will of an individual but only to the law. For Herodotus the vast slave populations on which the city-states of Greece were built simply did not exist. The same was true for every Greek or Roman citizen. Occasionally, but only occasionally, slaves surface briefly in the literature to remind us that beneath this rich and varied culture there were other peoples, other races who had made all this possible.

In antiquity slaves had come from all over the Greek and Roman worlds, from Syria, Egypt, Judaea, Dacia, Moesia, Germany, Gaul and Britain. They had performed many tasks.

Some had even occupied positions of considerable responsibility and relatively high social standing, which is probably why Odysseus believed that it was generally better in the world he knew to be a slave than a free labourer. The Romans had employed Greek slaves as tutors and household administrators. Athens in the fourth century BC was policed by a body of 300 Scythian archers who were slaves. Cicero's confidential secretary, who invented a form of shorthand which was named after him, was a slave called Tiro.[1] The Muslim world relied heavily on slave armies known as mamlûks, and in Egypt and Syria in the thirteenth century they succeeded in taking control of the state itself.

With the collapse of the Roman empire, however, this diversity rapidly vanished in the West. The Germanic peoples who overran the empire belonged to fragmentary societies with only limited engineering capabilities. Tribal in organization and nomadic or pastoral in origin, they were in no position either to acquire or to control the vast slave populations which had sustained the extensive building programmes, civic projects and complex urban lifestyles of those they had vanquished. In medieval Europe slaves were employed predominantly as agricultural labourers and supplemented a largely peasant workforce. In the end even field slavery was driven out by the spread of feudalism, the expansion of an agrarian economy and new agricultural technologies. Indentured peasants were easier to control than slaves and generally more productive. Slaves still continued to act as domestic servants; but within Europe at least, by the end of the Middle Ages the institution had ceased to fulfil any significant economic function.

Modern slavery was in many ways a new beginning and quite

unlike its ancient and medieval predecessors. It began on the morning of 8 August 1444 when the first cargo of 235 Africans, taken from what is now Senegal, was put ashore at the Portuguese port of Lagos. A rudimentary slave market was improvised on the docks and the confused and cowed Africans, reeling from weeks confined in the insalubrious holds of the tiny ships on which they had come, were herded into groups by age, sex and the state of their health. 'What heart could be so hard,' wrote the chronicler Gomes Eannes de Zurara who recorded the event,

> as not to be pierced with piteous feeling to see that company? Some held their heads low, their faces bathed in tears as they looked at each other; some groaned very piteously looking towards the heavens fixedly and crying out loud, as if they were calling on the father of the universe to help them. To increase their anguish still more, those who were in charge of the divisions then arrived and began to separate them one from another so that they formed five equal lots. This made it necessary to separate sons from their fathers and wives from their husbands, and brother from brother ... And as soon as the children who had been assigned to one group saw their parents in another they jumped up and ran towards them; mothers clasped their children in their arms and lay face downwards on the ground, accepting wounds with contempt for the suffering of their flesh rather than let their children be torn from them.

One person, it seems, who remained entirely unmoved was Prince Henry 'the Navigator' who had sponsored the voyage. He rode, according to Zurara, 'on a powerful horse accompanied by his people'. He extracted, as was his due, the royal fifth of all the sales – forty-six slaves in all – and then rode away. The traffic in 'Black Gold' had begun.[2]

The slaves sold that day would have found their way into private households in Portugal or on to private estates. But those who were to follow them in their hundreds of thousands were shipped not to Europe but across the Atlantic to the American colonies. Modern slavery was the creation of a new form of empire-building. It was developed to supply the manpower for a particular socio-economic unit – the sugar plantation – which had been unknown in the old world.[3] It was sugar which was responsible for the massive growth in the slave trade, between the fifteenth and eighteenth centuries, and it was the value of sugar to the economies of the slaving nations which made the abolition of slavery at the end of the eighteenth century such a protracted and uncertain business. As Daniel Defoe put it in 1713, 'No African Trade, no Negroes, No Negroes, No Sugar; no Sugar no Islands, no Islands no Continent, no Continent no Trade; that is to say farewell to your American Trade, your West Indian Trade.'

In its scale and its long-term consequences for population distribution – not to mention its sheer barbarity – it surpassed anything that had previously taken place. After the failure of the initial slave raids in Senegal and Senegambia, the Portuguese purchased their slaves from Africa and Arab middlemen. (Prince Henry justified this on the grounds that by buying slaves from Muslims he was turning their greed against them, and ultimately depriving them of vital manpower. Buy enough slaves, he argued, and the way would soon be open for a new Portuguese crusade against the African Infidel.) The slave trade had been endemic within Africa for centuries – a fact upon which its supporters tirelessly insisted. But the Europeans hugely increased the demand and by so doing encouraged African slavers to devastate whole areas and effectively exterminate entire peoples in the African hinterland. Europe, as the Marquis de Condorcet protested in 1781, 'is thus guilty not only of the crime of making slaves of men, but, on top of that, of all the slaughter committed in Africa in order to prepare for that crime'.[4]

The European demand for slaves transformed what had been a local commercial practice into the greatest forced migration in human history. Between 1492 and 1820 five or six times as many Africans went to America as did white Europeans. Modern slavery shattered entire cultures within Africa and built new ones on the far side of the Atlantic. It contributed to the creation of interracial communities, of Europeans and Africans, Africans and Native Americans, Asians and Africans, and it fragmented and dissipated communities which once were, or believed themselves to be, solidly endogamous. It also provided vast fortunes for those who lived by it and turned otherwise small, unremarkable seaports – Liverpool and Nantes, Bristol and Newport – into thriving, wealthy and sometimes sophisticated metropolises. It transformed small African communities such as Dahomey into powerful states. It made Brazil, the Caribbean and southern North America into multiracial societies in which Africans soon outnumbered the dwindling indigenous inhabitants or replaced them altogether.

Modern slavery was new, too, in its reliance upon a massive transatlantic trade. Trading in slaves had been a feature of both antiquity and the Middle Ages, and it had formed an important the Scandinavian economy between the eighth and eleventh centuries. But all of this was on a relatively small scale in comparison with the massive exportation of human merchandise that took place between the late sixteenth and early nineteenth centuries. Few had died in the ancient world as a consequence of the trade; countless millions perished during the infamous 'middle passage' between Africa and the Americas.[5]

Modern slavery also required a new conception of the relationship between slave and master. In antiquity slavery had been accepted as part of the order of the world. Some, such as Aristotle and Cicero, had tried to theorize the master-slave relationship as one between two types of persons: those who were naturally wise and masterful, and those who were naturally servile. But even Aristotle had been unable to distinguish clearly between the two. Natural slaves should, he argued, be everywhere robust, and natural rulers everywhere delicate and refined, 'making the one strong for servile labour, the other upright and although useless for service, useful for the political life in the arts of both peace and war'. Yet he was forced to concede that 'the opposite frequently happens – that some have the souls and others the bodies of freemen'.[6] Nature, it would seem, is not always able to fulfil her own intentions. The idea, however, had a rich afterlife. It was much used by the Spanish in America, and employed in a slightly modified, more emphatically biological form in the nineteenth century by both the British in Australia and the French in Africa.[7]

In practice, however, one became a slave in antiquity as a 'punishment' for having fought on the losing side in a war. (Unwanted children who had been exposed by their parents could also be enslaved, although this does not seem to have happened very often.) Those who were defeated in battle were generally slain, those who were not were 'saved', the price of their salvation being enslavement. As late as 1804, one of opponents of the abolitionists, William Devyanes, a former Chairman of the East India Company, following the same general logic, proposed that the slave trade could be defended on the grounds that 'if the slave merchants did not purchase from him and others, their prisoners taken in war would be killed'.

The triumph of Christianity made very little difference to this view. Both the Old Testament and the Qur'an accepted that it was legitimate to enslave individuals, and indeed entire populations, in the pursuit of supposedly just wars, and there is nothing in the gospels to contradict this. The church did attempt to restrict the degree to which Christians might themselves be enslaved by other Christians, but was prepared to countenance the enslavement of Christians by non-Christians. (Martin Luther even warned Christian slaves against 'stealing themselves' away from their Muslim masters.)

The vast majority of modern slaves, and all those employed on the plantations in America, were Africans who had clearly not been acquired in a 'just' war. How then could such enslavement possibly be legitimate? Some early attempts were made by the Portuguese, the Spanish and the French to argue that the African internal warfare of which they were the beneficiaries, and which they had, if not created, certainly greatly exacerbated, had itself been 'just'. When in 1546 the Spanish theologian Francisco de Vitoria, who was otherwise so severe in his criticism of the Spanish occupation of America, was asked about the moral validity of the Portuguese claim to have purchased slaves who had been taken in a 'just' African war, he replied that it was not up to the slavers to discover 'the justice of wars between barbarians'. All they needed was the assurance of the traders that the human merchandise they were buying had been legitimately acquired, 'and they may be bought without a qualm'.[8] Needless to say, when they were called upon to do so the African slavers were all too happy to provide such assurances, although they must have found the European need for them deeply puzzling.

Few, however, found such arguments very convincing. Between 1684 and 1686 the Holy Office (the papal Inquisition) received a number of petitions, mostly from a Portuguese mulatto named Lourenço da Silva, denouncing such self-serving justifications of the trade. Da Silva's initiative received considerable support from the Capuchin order whose missionary efforts in the Congo had been constantly thwarted by the slave-traders. In 1686 the Holy Office actually went so far as to condemn the slave trade (although not slavery as such). Since it took no action against the slavers themselves, the injunction was wholly ignored. But it did give some moral weight to the opponents of the trade; and some of Da Silva's arguments, in particular that free peoples of colour should be treated just as free whites, may have inspired the French *Code noir* of 1688. This remained in force in the French overseas possessions until the revolution and, although on most issues it followed the Roman law on slavery, it did guarantee at least in theory a greater measure of independence to slaves than existed in any of the other European colonies.

As protests against slavery and the slave trade in particular mounted, it became increasingly difficult to find any sustainable argument for its existence. Neither the just war thesis nor any kind of racism could finally stand up to close examination. The conviction that the slave was some kind of lesser being ran counter to the very nature of the master-slave relationship, which demanded of slaves a far higher degree of comprehension and rational calculation than were possessed by the domestic animals after which, in a sustained attempt to deny the obvious fact of their humanity, their masters frequently named them: Jumper, Juno, Fido, and so on. Slaves could, after all, breed with their masters – a persistent fear in slave-holding societies. They could converse with their masters; they could even, as Benjamin Franklin observed, unlike sheep, rise in revolt against their masters.

For a convinced Christian, there was always the claim that although the slave might be constituted like any other human being, Africans knew nothing of Christianity before they were enslaved. Slavery, therefore, had saved them from eternal damnation. No matter how appalling the slaves' condition might be – and many claimed to believe that it was in fact no worse than that of day-labourers in Europe – it was far better for their minds and their souls to be enslaved among civilized beings than free among their own savage kind. What was a little suffering and privation in this world in comparison with hell-fire in the next? Zurara might have been somewhat disingenuous when he claimed that Prince Henry's 'entire riches' lay not in the forty-six slaves he had taken in August 1444 but in the certainty 'of the salvation of those souls which had before been lost', but he was in effect stating what in the following centuries was to become a commonplace. The philosopher John Locke, who passionately denounced slavery as 'so vile and miserable an estate of Man, and so directly opposed to the Generous Temper and Spirit of our Nation' that ' 'tis hardly to be conceived that an *Englishman* much less a *Gentleman* would plead for it', nevertheless held shares in the Royal Africa Company, the main business of which was the slave trade, and defended slavery for Africans on the ground that it rescued them from the worse fate of barbarism and eternal damnation. Even the seventeenth-century Jesuit Antonio de Vieira, who was one of the very few to speak openly against all forms of slavery, transformed the sufferings of the Indians in Brazil into a vocation which had 'illuminated' them and for which they would receive 'eternal inheritance as a reward'. 'Oh what a change of fortune,' he told them, 'will be yours at that time, and what astonishment and confusion for those who have so little humanity today!'

What is missing from Zurara's account and even from Vieira's indignation, what is missing from nearly all the pleas for the abolition of slavery before the middle of the eighteenth century, is the awareness that suffering is a human universal. Because the curious creatures Zurara had seen on the docks at Lagos could suffer as he could they must indeed be human, and their humanity necessarily imposed an obligation to alleviate it. There are, after all, many better ways of becoming Christian.

The slave's right to freedom of choice, even the right to select his or her own forms of indebtedness – which most clearly distinguished the slave from the European day-labourer – was a mode, as Diderot phrased it, of 'an enjoyment in one's own mind' to which all human beings are entitled. The slave, denied this feature of what it is to be a person, was thus reduced to a level lower even than that of the dogs which the Spaniards had brought with them to America. For the dog is only an auto-maton, whereas the slave still retains some grasp on what nothing can deprive him of, his consciousness. He or she alone *knows* that he or she is a slave. Only the slave among living beings has been denied all cause for hope, all expectation of what Diderot called 'those happy times, those centuries of Enlightenment and of prosperity' which might one day allow even the most miserable labourer to recover his identity to the full.

In the end, it was humanitarian arguments such as these which brought the whole business to an end – that and the fact that by the mid-eighteenth century the slave trade had begun to be far less profitable than it had once been.[9] Yet even the abolitionists, while they loathed both the trade and the institution, still clung firmly to a belief in the civilizing potential of European culture. William Wilberforce, the most outspoken, dogged and successful of them, remained convinced that emancipating the Africans might ultimately be less important than bringing 'the reign of light and truth and happiness among them', by which he meant primarily Christianity and British 'laws, institutions and manners'.

The abolitionists recognized that as humans the Africans had an absolute right to freedom, but this did not make them the equal of the Europeans, nor did it exempt them from certain kinds of tutelage. Claims for the inferiority of the African and the consequent rights of the European to long-term tutelage remained a significant ideological prop for the European overseas empires in the nineteenth century. They had, and in some areas continue to have, a determining impact on the modern relationship between the developed and developing worlds.

Slavery of any formal kind – for there are many informal kinds still in existence – came to an end in the territories of the European overseas empires during the first decades of the nineteenth century. The first European state to outlaw the slave trade was Denmark in 1792. British involvement in the trade ended in 1805–7 and by 1824 slaving had become a capital offence. The African reaction to all this was, predictably, one of bewilderment. Why, the King of the Ashanti asked a British official in 1820, had his people sudden stopped buying slaves when the Muslims continued to do so? Were not their Gods the same and if the Qur'an did not forbid slavery why was it that the Bible had suddenly begun to do so? He received no answer.

Together with the attempts to outlaw the trade, the Western powers had also made a number of sporadic attempts to return some of the victims of the trade if not exactly to their homes then at least to Africa. In 1792 a settlement duly named Freetown had been created on the Sierra Leone peninsula in West Africa by a group of British philanthropists to provide a new home for escaped or liberated slaves. After 1808 Freetown became in effect a British colony and its harbour provided the base for the British warships which patrolled the West African coast in search of slave-traders. During the next sixty years the original population of Freetown was increased by some 60,000 men, women and children who had been freed from captured slave ships.[10] Similar settlements, although far smaller and less successful, were established by the French at Libreville on the estuary of the Gabon in 1839–48, and by private American initiatives on the Grain Coast (modern Liberia) in 1821.

By the end of 1870 the trade worldwide was effectively at an end. (The last verified landing was in Cuba in January of that year.) Slavery, however, survived in Brazil until 1888, and it was not until 1890 that the General Act of Brussels committed the European colonial powers in Africa to stamp it out in their territories. In doing so they transformed the abolition of an institution which had for so long been the mainstay of their overseas empires into a part of their own 'civilizing mission'.[11]

Slavery was officially at an end. A painful period in human history, which had lasted for millennia, had been, or so it seemed, extinguished. In 1890 the Brazilian abolitionist Rui Barbosa ordered all the papers in the Ministry of the Treasury relating to slavery to be publicly burned. Among those who turned out to watch this conflagration was a worker in the customhouse, who claimed to be 108 years old. He had come, he said, to witness for himself the 'complete destruction' of the documents which contained the history of the 'martyrdom' of his race.[12] He could never perhaps have imagined that his race was also about to enter upon another kind of martyrdom, one which would not only lead to other kinds of divisions and conflicts in almost all the societies which had once benefited from the African slave trade, but which would also lead to seemingly endemic civil war within Africa itself.

9 The final frontier

The fight against slavery began in the middle years of the eighteenth century as Britain was in the process of losing one empire and acquiring another. It began, too, at the same time as a quite different development in the long history of the relationship between peoples. By this period most of the earth's surface had been explored, charted and in some cases colonized by Europeans. Most parts, that is, except one: the Pacific. The Pacific had, of course, been crossed and recrossed many times since the circumnavigation by the fleet which set out in 1519 under the command of Magellan. But for Europeans it remained a largely uncharted mystery, the imprecise location of 'the unknown southern land', the very existence of which comprised (along with the Northwest Passage) the last remaining geographical myth. In the eighteenth century the Pacific became the final frontier.

The fantasies that since antiquity had plagued or delighted the European imagination had been moving steadily further and further away from Europe itself. The marvels and monsters with which the ancients had populated the globe but which had failed to turn up in Europe, Africa or 'Ethiopia' were later found in 'India' or, after 1492, in America. In 1512 Juan Ponce de León went to Florida in search of the fountain of eternal youth, and Francisco de Orellana was so convincing in his description of the Amazons that he had seen there that their name, not his, was given to the great river that he was the first to navigate.

The horizon of these possibilities began to recede, however, with the advance of modern science which made increasingly improbable such curiosities as men with their faces in the middle of their chests or with one large foot which they raised over their heads at noon to protect themselves from the sun. By the time first the British, then the French and Spanish, began to explore the South Pacific no one believed any longer in such things. They did, however, still believe in something else perhaps no less chimerical. They believed that somewhere in the world there existed lands where nature provided all that humankind required, and where peoples lived wholly virtuous lives free from the terrible constraints of civilization. This vision, part fantasy and part ethnographic curiosity, was loosely based upon impressionistic travellers' tales. It was a transposed version of the dream of the earthly paradise or what in antiquity were called the Islands of the Blest. Alexander had visited it, in myth if not in reality, and it had been glimpsed briefly by eager European readers in Amerigo Vespucci's account of America – until that was shown to be a forgery. Thomas More's *Utopia* (1516), which claims to be an account by one of Vespucci's sailors, is in part at least a satire on the possibility that any such place could exist in reality.

In 1766 a French nobleman, mathematician and explorer named Antoine de Bougainville left Nantes on the frigate *La Boudeuse* with instructions to observe the transit of Venus (a means of measuring the distance of the earth from the sun) – a somewhat ironic commission in the circumstances – and if possible to complete a circumnavigation of the globe. The fol-

lowing year he joined up with *L'Étoile* off the Malvinas/
Falklands and headed out into the Pacific. On the morning of
4 April 1768 he landed on an island where, he later declared,
'one might think oneself in the Elysian Fields'. It had a perfect
climate (untroubled, he noticed immediately, by the fearsome
insects which infest most tropical paradises), an abundance of
food which required no cultivation, and was inhabited by a
people who seemed to have no social organization, possessed
only a rudimentary religion, and lived together as one large
family. Not only were they happy and peaceful, they were also
beautiful, more beautiful than anything to be seen in Europe.
'The men are six feet or more,' he wrote, 'and better proportioned
and better made than any I have ever encountered; no painter
could find a finer model for a Hercules or a Mars.' All of them,
even the aged, had 'the most beautiful teeth in the world' – no
small virtue in the eighteenth century when few people over
the age of thirty could count many of their own. (The botanist
Sir Joseph Banks, who visited the island the following year,
noted in much the same tone of surprise that their breath was
'entirely free from any disagreeable smell'.)

But it was the women who really caught Bougainville's attention and that of his crew. They were beautiful, unadorned and
entirely natural. The contours of their bodies in particular had,
as he observed, 'not been disfigured by fifty years of torture', a
reference to the constraining corsets into which most women
in Europe were strapped. Above all, 'their sole passion is love
... sweet indolence and the concern to please is their most
serious occupation'. Jealousy was apparently unknown among
them, and 'all are encouraged to follow the inclinations of their
hearts or the law of their senses, and are publicly applauded for

doing so. The air they breathe, their songs, their dances, which are almost always accompanied with lascivious gestures, all speak at every moment of the pleasures of love.' 'These people,' Bougainville concluded, 'live only in the tranquillity and the pleasure of the senses.' Because of this he called the place 'The New Cythera', after the island in the Peloponnese on which Venus had been born. We, of course, know it as Tahiti.'

In 1771 Bougainville published an account of his voyage, the *Voyage autour du monde*, which became a bestseller. This, and a letter by the surgeon of *La Boudeuse*, Philibert Commerson, which had appeared in the *Mercure de France* the year before, established Tahiti as an exotic – and erotic – paradise. Thereafter it became the final resting place of the myth of the 'noble savage'. For Bougainville, and later for Diderot who wrote a review of the *Voyage autour du monde* and a famous (and fictional) supplement to it, the Tahitians seemed as no other 'primitive' people had before to provide proof that somewhere in the world it was possible to live wholly fulfilled lives beyond the reach of religious dogma, laws or social conventions. In Bougainville's account Tahiti was a place without warfare or hardships. It was a place in which humankind's better instincts had not, as Diderot expressed it, been smothered by those of the 'artificial man' which European civilization had created in their stead.

Most of this, as Bougainville himself later came to recognize, was either misleading or simply false. The Tahitians were by no means unwarlike, nor did they lack either social laws or deeply-held religious beliefs. The dedication of the women to 'sweet indolence and the concern to please' was real enough, but it derived from a set of social practices and expectations no less rigid than those that in France compelled women to behave in quite other ways. Yet for all that, the Tahitians were undeniably untainted by contact with Europeans, came closer to meeting European aesthetic expectations than most other 'primitive' peoples and were certainly far more exotic than anything that had been seen since Columbus made his first landfall in 1492.

Bougainville made Tahiti famous throughout Europe. In the years that followed his voyage, British and French ships would sail across the entire length and breadth of the Pacific Ocean until virtually every island had been mapped and in most cases formally, if only fleetingly, 'possessed' by one or another of the European powers. The most celebrated of these voyages were those made under the patronage of the Royal Society by Captain James Cook between 1768 and 1778. Like Bougainville, Cook had gone to the Pacific to observe the transit of Venus and, while doing so to observe, map and record. Like Bougainville, too, though more restrained in his enthusiasms, he saw the Polynesians as living lives very close to those which all humankind must have lived before being transformed by 'civilization'. The Pacific Ocean thus became a kind of living anthropological laboratory, 'a fit soil', as John Douglas described it in the preface he wrote for the official account of Captain Cook's third voyage, 'from whence a careful observer could collect facts for forming a judgement, how far human nature will be apt to degenerate, and in what respects it can ever be able to excel'. What he termed the 'novelties of the Society or Sandwich Islands' were a record of the whole of humankind in its infancy.[2]

Bougainville and Cook enjoyed cordial, even amicable, relationships with these samples of early humankind, in so far, that is, as they were able to control their crews – not an easy task, as both men noted, with a gang of sex-starved males confronted with hordes of women whose sole passion was 'love ... sweet indolence and the concern to please'. But as with all such contacts, relationships soon became strained as more and more navigators visited the islands. The much publicized death of Cook himself in Hawaii on his third voyage in 1778, of Marion de Fresne in New Zealand in 1772, and the slaughter of twelve of the companions of the French navigator La Pérouse on Samoa, darkened the vision of the noble, gentle savage. 'No person,' wrote La Pérouse on his return, 'can imagine the Indians of the South Seas to be in a savage state. On the contrary they must have made very great progress in civilization, and I believe them to be as corrupt as the circumstances they are placed in will allow them to be.'

Yet for all that, Bougainville's elegiac and Cook's somewhat more matter-of-fact descriptions of their encounters with the Tahitians created an enduring image of the Pacific as a place where it was possible to act out all the European fantasies of sexual freedom and complete liberty from social constraint. It was an image that was still powerful enough over a hundred years later to persuade the painter Paul Gauguin to abandon home, family and a secure job for a life in the South Seas. There he found, alas, a very different Tahiti, riven by European disease, its tranquillity turned to despair by Christian missionaries.

The Pacific islands were not, however, merely the rococo pleasure grounds that Bougainville's and Commerson's descriptions had made of them. They were also revictualling places for European merchant ships and potential stages on the route to the fabled southern continent, should it exist. Both France and

Britain, watched anxiously by Spain which still looked upon the Pacific as its own special sphere of influence, had vague but quite evident designs on the potential riches of the southern ocean. Since the end of the Seven Years War the French, in particular the circles around the influential duc de Choiseul and the Ministère de la Marine et Colonies, had begun to think about the possibility of a French overseas empire in the Pacific.

For some optimistic spirits in France, the Pacific seemed to hold out the promise of a new kind of imperialism, one which would truly benefit equally the colonizer and the colonized. As early as 1756, even before the loss of Canada, the influential polymath Charles de Brosses had set out a project for a new kind of settlement in the Pacific which would, he hoped, compensate for what the Europeans had done to the Americas. 'Imagine,' he wrote,

> a future which is not at all like that which Christopher Columbus secured for our neighbours ... For we would avoid the two vices from which the Spaniards then suffered, avarice and cruelty. The former emptied their own country in pursuit of an illusory fortune, something which should never have been attempted. The latter, whose causes were national pride and superstition, has all but destroyed the human race in America. They massacred disdainfully, and as if they were base and alien beasts, millions of Indians whom they could have made into men.

No longer, insisted De Brosses, could the Europeans aspire to 'establishing imaginary kingdoms beyond the equator'. Like the empire which Burke had hoped to see in India, De Brosses' enlightened French presence in the Pacific would combine trade with education. It would purchase from the 'savages' the hardwoods and pearls which the Europeans required and in time, through the benign influence of commerce, the Polynesians would come to see 'the advantages of human and social laws'. The model for all future French empires, concluded De Brosses, should be not the Spaniards or the Romans but the Phoenicians. For the Phoenicians, as a peaceful trading people, had created not dependencies or colonies but new nations, and 'what greater objective could a sovereign have' than that?[3]

This vision was shared by many later French writers, by Diderot and the Abbé Guillaume Raynal in particular. But despite the enthusiasm which greeted the Pacific voyages, it was to remain only a vision. In the sands of Tahiti, Bougainville had planted a wooden plaque, together with a bottle containing the names of all the officers on his three ships, which declared this and all Polynesia to be French territory. (Two years earlier, however, the English navigator Samuel Wallis had visited the island and renamed it, rather more prosaically, 'King George's Island'.) No attempt was ever made to make good this claim. After the creation of the French republic in 1792 the revolutionary government turned its back on any future colonizing ventures – until, that is, the creation of the Napoleonic empire. When Tahiti was finally established as a French colony in 1880 after having been devastated by Protestant missionaries, European traders and beachcombers for nearly a century, the vision of enlightened co-operation between over-civilized Europeans and simple 'noble savages' in which, as Diderot had hoped, each might learn from the other, had been entirely forgotten.

Like Bougainville, Cook was also involved in plans for some future occupation of the Pacific. James Douglas, Earl of Morton and President of the Royal Society, provided him with a set of 'Hints' as to how he was to conduct his voyage. These warned him in the strongest terms against doing anything that would cause harm to the natives, and roundly condemned any form of colonization. He was cautioned, 'To have it still in view that shedding the blood of these people is a crime of the highest nature. They are human creatures, the work of the same omnipotent Author, equally under His care with the most polished European; perhaps being less offensive more entitled to His favour. They are the natural, and in the strict sense of the word, the legal possessors of the several Regions they inhabit.'4 Cook also carried with him, however, a set of 'Instructions' marked 'Secret' and given to him by the Admiralty. These were rather less interested in science and rather more in the possibilities of future imperial expansion. Cook was similarly advised against any conflict but he was also told to 'take possession of Convenient Situations in the Country in the name of the King of Great Britain' and to 'take Possession for his Majesty by setting up Proper Marks and inscriptions, as first discoverers and possessors'.

Yet for all this it would be a mistake to see any of these early expeditions as merely covert colonizing operations. For one thing neither Bougainville's nor Cook's ships had been designed for such purposes. All were shallow-draught vessels, lightly armed and built for working close inshore. Then there is a wholly different sensibility in Bougainville's and Cook's accounts of their encounters with the Polynesians from that found in any of the travel narratives that preceded them. Both men talk of the Polynesians with wonder and sometimes incredulity, but also with respect and even at times with a kind of baffled affection. Nowhere is settlement ever seriously envisaged, even in Cook's supposedly nefarious secret instructions, except with the express 'Consent of the Natives' and even then only 'if you find the Country uninhabited'. Cook himself refused to do even this. In the journal of his final voyage he remarked that the Tahitians had shown him 'with what facility a settlement might be made at Otaheite, which grateful as I am for their repeated good offers, I hope will never happen'.[5] Bougainville and Cook carried back to Europe a greater knowledge of the extent and nature of the South Pacific. They returned with data, calculations and charts. They came carrying specimens of minerals and plants. Both also returned with people, living human specimens of the diversity of humankind.

When Bougainville arrived in Paris in May 1769, he was accompanied by a Tahitian he called Aotourou. Aotourou had joined the French fleet of his own free will in order to accompany it home and to see the wonders that France had to offer. (Since he assumed, not unreasonably, that France was a nearby island he can have had no idea of the length or the kind of journey on which he had embarked.) In Paris, he became something of a celebrity. He was welcomed into the circle of the duchesse de Choiseul, taken to the Opéra and the zoo, paraded in the Tuileries and introduced to various salons where he met some of the leading scientists and philosophers of the day. Among others, he was scrutinized by the natural historian Buffon; the explorer of the Amazon, Charles de la Condamine, who later wrote an account of his visit; Diderot, who in a fiction entitled *Supplément au voyage de Bougainville* transformed him into a harsh critic of the irrationality of Christian moral laws; the philosophers Helvétius and Holbach. He was examined by a celebrated French phonetician to discover why his language sounded the way it did and why he had failed to learn French. He may even have been presented to the king. His one defect, it seems (apart from his failure to master French), was his ugliness. Bougainville recorded with irritation that the *beau monde* of Paris persisted in asking why, 'from an island where the men are generally so beautiful I should have chosen someone so ugly'. To which Bougainville replied that 'I repeat once and for all that I did not choose him, he chose me.' Bougainville also insisted that Aotourou made up in intelligence for what he lacked in looks – although since he was never able to master French and there is no suggestion that Bougainville ever learnt a word of Tahitian, how the two men communicated is unclear.

Aotourou was a specimen, but he was treated as a human being, a curious and puzzling human being perhaps, an object of scientific inquiry, but a human being nonetheless. No attempt was even made to convert him to Christianity. Finally he was sent home (at the by now bankrupt Bougainville's own expense), carrying gifts from the king and the duc de Choiseul, but he died of measles en route in November 1771. Three years later, when he returned from his second voyage, Captain Cook also brought back a native, this time from Huahine in the Sandwich Islands (now Hawaii). Although Cook seems to have had a low opinion of his intellect, based largely on his failure to be impressed by the splendours of London, Mai, or Omai as he came to be called, was undoubtedly handsome. He, too, became a celebrity. He had his portrait painted by Reynolds, in which he appears dressed in a belted version of a toga and in the traditional pose of the Roman orator, and by William Parry. He proved to be a great favourite at court and became the subject of several popular plays.

Omai returned home on board the *Resolution* on Cook's third and last voyage in 1776. Like Aotourou, he was given a number of what might seem to be inappropriate gifts: a sword presented to him by Joseph Banks who had had himself painted with Omai, and a suit of armour from Lord Sandwich which had been made specially by the armourers of the Tower of London.[6] These and a number of other more useful items Cook hoped 'would be the means of rising him into consequence, and of making him respected, and even courted by the first persons throughout the extent of the Society Islands'. On finally reaching Huahine on 13 October 1777, Omai was set up in a new house negotiated for him by Cook and given a number of European weapons (about which Cook had some misgivings) together with a horse and mare, a goat 'big with kid', a boar and two sows 'of the English breed', and a number of European plants. Omai took his leave of Cook on the deck of the *Resolution* and wept all the way to the shore. As Cook put out to sea he wrote in his journal that, 'It was no small satisfaction to reflect, that we had brought him safe back to the very spot from which he was taken. And yet such is the strange nature of human affairs, that it is probable that we left him in a less desirable situation than he was in before his connection with us.' What became of him after that we do not know since, as Cook somewhat wistfully concluded, that was a matter for 'the future navigators of this ocean; with whom it cannot be a principal object of curiosity to trace the future fortunes of our traveller'.

Cook had brought Omai back home. He had also brought with him, in addition to the animals he had given to Omai, some horses, goats and cows with which he hoped the islanders might be able to improve what he (unlike Bougainville) saw as their restricted and impoverished diet. It was, as he conceived it, an act of simple magnanimity – evidence, as had been the repatriation of Omai, of the Europeans' goodwill. 'The trouble and vexation that attended bringing this living cargo thus far,' he recorded, 'is hardly to be conceived. But the satisfaction of mind that I felt in having been so fortunate as to fulfil his Majesty's humane design in sending such valuable animals to supply the wants of two worthy nations, sufficiently recompensed me for the many anxious hours I had passed.'[7] We are a long way from Columbus, on the island he called Hispaniola, trading pieces of glass and 'other trinkets of little worth' for gold and silver ornaments.

Contact between the Europeans and these 'two worthy nations' was, nonetheless, not entirely disinterested. The offspring of Cook's cattle would serve later generations of European sailors well. Cook's reticence to settle would not be followed by later, less considerate generations. Soon the missionaries and the merchants arrived, and after them came the colonizers, first British, then French and finally, with the annexation of Hawaii in 1893, American.

During the late eighteenth century an astonishing number of voyages of exploration left from various parts of Europe, few if any of which had obvious colonizing intentions. Charles de la Condamine travelled down the Amazon in 1743 and 1744 in a voyage which was a joint French–Spanish venture. The Portuguese Xavier Ribeiro de Sampaio left the following year for the Rio Negro. Nicolas le Caille went to observe the transit of

Mercury from the Cape of Good Hope in 1751. La Pérouse followed Bougainville into the Pacific in 1785. In 1789, Alejandro Malaspina set out to chart all the possessions claimed by the Spanish crown, 'in the wake of Messrs Cook and La Pérouse', and to prove to the world at large that Spain was every bit as enlightened a nation as France and Britain.

All these expeditions carried botanists, engineers, hydrographers, physicists, physicians, astronomers and painters, but very few soldiers and no missionaries. Even the names of their ships were intended to reflect their purpose: *Discovery*, *Resolution*, *Adventure* and *Endeavour*; *Géographie* and *Naturaliste*; L'Astrolabe and *La Boussole* (compass). They were something new in the history of empires and the peoples who created them. They represented the point at which the pursuit of power and the pursuit of knowledge met. 'Abstract science, Gentlemen,' La Roncière la Noury, President of the Paris Geographical Society, told its members in 1874, 'is not sufficient to serve humanity. Science is not truly fruitful unless it is the instrument of progress and production.'

Some of these scientific ventures, such as the expedition in 1735–6 under Louis Godin to test Newton's hypothesis about the shape of the globe, were devoid of any secondary purposes; some, in the manner of the Pacific voyages, had mixed objectives. Others, like the great ordnance survey carried out by the British in India between 1765 and 1843, served quite specific political ends. All were intended to enhance the reputation of the nation both at home and abroad. When Bougainville's account of his journey appeared in 1771, Johann Reinhold Forster (who later accompanied Cook to the Pacific) rapidly made a translation of it because, he said, 'Every true patriot would wish that the East India Company would imitate the French' and 'despatch men properly acquainted with mathematics, natural history [and] physic' to discover 'new branches of trade and commerce'.

Competition between the European powers had acquired an extra and, with the rapid spread of industrialization, potentially more sinister dimension. Science became a recognized source of power and a terrain on which the European powers fought one another for pre-eminence. It might be fanciful to see this as similar to the space-race between the world's most recent empires, the United States and the Soviet Union, in the mid-twentieth century – fanciful, but not entirely wrong. As with the space-race, military advantage, or in the case of the Pacific the possibility of colonization, was a secondary consideration. What mattered most was national prestige. The disinterested pursuit of science was transformed into a new kind of ideology, and the scientist became a new kind of hero.

After Cook was killed in Hawaii in 1779 he became not merely yet another casualty of the dangerous business of seafaring but a martyr to science and a new vision of empire. All of the many tributes paid to him, which were published in French and Italian as well as English, contrasted his deeds with those of the older heroes of empire: Alexander, Scipio, Cortés and Pizarro. They had only conquered men and destroyed peoples in doing so. Cook, enthused the Italian Michelangelo Gianetti in a eulogy published by the Royal Academy of Florence in 1785, had cleared the seas of terror and embraced rather than slaughtered those whom he had encountered in the Pacific. In doing so, he had carried the banner of 'an Enlightened Monarch and Enlightened Society' around the earth. Philip James de Loutherbourg's engraving of 1794, *The Apotheosis of Captain James Cook*, shows him being transported aloft by the figures of Britannia and Universal Fame. In keeping with ancient Greek practice, he is a hero who has been transformed into a god. Nothing could capture so neatly the alliance of science and empire, which had first been dreamt up by the mythologizers of Alexander the Great and would endure until the end of empire itself.[8]

10 *Empire, race and nation*

Cook's triumph, as his panegyrists made plain, had been the triumph not only of science but also of the British nation. The imperialism which he represented was the creation of a new mode of identity and political creed, one that has done more than any other to shape the world since the early nineteenth century: nationalism. Nationalism is the idea that peoples have separate, distinct and indissoluble features, that they are united by a common language and culture, and live under a single and indigenous ruler. When it first emerged at the end of the eighteenth century, this creed made the older empires of the world look like doomed attempts to prevent the evolution of national, and natural, human features.

The German philosopher Johann Gottfried von Herder (1744–1803), who is often somewhat unjustly identified as the father of German and hence most European nationalism, argued that 'Nature has separated nations, not only by woods and mountains, seas and deserts, rivers and climates, but most particularly by languages, inclinations and characters, that the work of subjugating despotism might be rendered more difficult, that all the four quarters of the globe might not be crammed into the belly of a wooden horse.'[1] The use of force and economic interest might have temporarily 'glued together' the world's empires into 'fragile machines of state' but underneath this apparatus they were all, he insisted, 'destitute of internal unification and sympathy of parts'. For Herder the concepts of a people – a *Volk* – and an empire were simply incompatible. Sooner or later all the world's empires – those 'Trojan Horses' as he called them, which conspired against the natural plurality of the human race – were destined to collapse back into their constituent parts. The colonists and settlers would either be driven out or would in time become absorbed by the indigenous peoples. In this way 'does not Nature revenge every insult offered her?'[2]

But the European empires proved to be far more adaptable and a good deal more amorphous than Herder had allowed for. Far from disappearing with the rise of the nation, all the great empires of the nineteenth century, the French and the British in particular, were created in its shadow. Since antiquity empire has been one way of uniting a people. It had after all, as Aristotle observed, been the people of Athens, the *demos*, and not the better sort, the *aristoi*, who had been responsible for the growth of the Athenian empire. And as we have already seen, in his struggle with the tribune Naevius, Scipio Africanus was able to appeal to the Roman people in the name of 'their' empire. Profitable adventures beyond the boundaries of the homeland have always been a way for rulers to give their subjects what Machiavelli shrewdly called 'great expectation of themselves' – one way of making them forget if only briefly their present divisions and miseries. Only as long as Rome was expanding, as Machiavelli also observed, had she been free from corruption. When she stopped, her peoples fell to squabbling among themselves and instantly lost the martial spirit which had held the state together.

Similar uses of the images of empire and the greatness it

evoked were made by later generations of Europeans. Nowhere is this more striking, and nowhere perhaps has it had more lasting consequences, than in France. In the immediate aftermath of the revolution, when France was surrounded on all sides by enemies and internally disunited, 'The Empire' or 'Our Empire' came to denote the personality of the entire French nation. It stood very much as it had once done throughout Europe for the unification of disparate local groups into a single whole. An empire was understood to be not the rule of a single individual but a federation entered into voluntarily. 'Emperor,' declared one enthusiast in the 1790s, 'means he who rules over a free people.' The title King by contrast, as the Romans had known, meant only 'tyrant'.[3] 'We are always hearing about the great empire of the whole nation,' mocked the French liberal Benjamin Constant in 1815, 'abstract notions which have no reality. The great empire is nothing independently of its provinces. The whole nation is nothing separated from the parts that compose it.'

Constant, however, was writing after the collapse of Napoleon whom he abhorred. Napoleon, in his view, by welding abstractions into the instruments of tyranny, had attempted to cast the nation in his own image. When, on 12 December 1804, Napoleon had himself crowned by Pope Pius VII he formally assumed the role that the Holy Roman emperor had once held. As Consul for Life of the republic, he took the crown from the pope and placed it on his head himself. This famous gesture was more than simple hubris. It embodied the claim that as the supreme representative of the people he was the only person who could effect the transition from republic to empire. Like Charlemagne, whose crown he now wore and who had called himself the

Father of the Europeans, Napoleon's first ambition was to unify a Europe which he saw as one people broken down 'by revolutions and politics'. His idea, he wrote from his final exile on St Helena, had been 'to bring everywhere unity of laws, of principles, of opinions, sentiments, views and interests. Then perhaps it would have been possible to dream for the great European family, the application of the American Congress or of the Amphictyons of Greece.'

The Greek Amphictyonic Council, which had previously inspired both James Madison's image of the future United States in the 1770s and Immanuel Kant's vision of a global cosmopolitan order in the 1790s, had been a loose federation of city-states dedicated to the protection of the temple of Demeter at Anthela near Thermopylae. It did not correspond very closely to the image that many had of the Napoleonic empire, in particular those who were drawn unwillingly and by force into its orbit. But there was a logic in Napoleon's objectives which ran back to the universalistic aspirations expressed in the Declaration of the Rights of Man of 1789. This had set out 'the fundamental principles which must provide the ground for all government' and had gone on to declare that 'the French people [were] the first of all peoples and a model for every nation', or as Napoleon himself later put it rather more bluntly, '*Ce qui est bon pour les français est bon pour tout le monde*' (What is good for the French is good for everybody).

For Napoleon a unified Europe with France at its head was to be only the first step. In his own personal mythology Napoleon was not only the heir to Charlemagne but had also taken up the diadem of Alexander and with it had assumed the historic task of uniting East and West. The first and, as it transpired, the last people to be caught up in this piece of historical mythologizing were the Egyptians. When Napoleon arrived in Egypt in 1798 – significantly on board a ship called *L'Orient* – he came, he claimed, as Alexander had come to the peoples of Bactria, not as a conqueror but as a liberator. More immediately he also hoped that by occupying Egypt he would damage British trade in the eastern Mediterranean and threaten British India. Despite these obvious military objectives, the invasion was certainly unusual. No one else had ever gone on campaign with an entire scientific academy, the Institut d'Égypte. Part conquest, part exploration, the purpose of the Egyptian expedition was to restore a state of true civility to the 'Orient'.

In the words of the massive *Description de l'Égypte* which appeared in twenty-three volumes between 1809 and 1828, and each page of which measured one metre square, Egypt which had 'transmitted its knowledge to so many nations' was now under its Mamlûk and Ottoman rulers 'plunged into barbarism'. From this unhappy condition Napoleon, the 'Mohammed of the West', as Victor Hugo later called him, had come to release it and while he was there to 'make the lives of the inhabitants more pleasant and to procure for them all the advantages of a perfect civilization'.[4] This civilization was to be predominantly French. Yet it was also to be a civilization which would preserve, as had Alexander's, what the French looked upon as the true spirit of the Orient, in this case the wisdom of the Pharaohs in happy alliance with the pieties of Islam. In Napoleon's view it was the French, despite being Christians, and not the Mamlûks who, by restoring to the Egyptians their cultural inheritance, were 'the true Muslims'. In order to get this point across, everything the Armée d'Égypte did was explained and justified in precise Qur'anic Arabic, and when the Mohammed of the West departed, he gave strict instructions to his deputy, Jean-Baptise Kléber, to administer Cairo in co-operation with the members of the Institut d'Égypte and local religious leaders.

The occupation did not, however, last long. In June 1801, after a series of battles with local rulers, the Ottomans and the British, the French were finally driven out by a combined British and Ottoman assault. By 1814 Napoleon himself was in exile on the island of Elba, defeated by the combined forces of Russia, Austria, Prussia and Britain and the disillusionment of his own exhausted peoples. His return the following year was spectacular but brief and doomed. On 18 June 1815 at the Battle of Waterloo the new Alexander and with him the vision of a world united beneath the principles of the French revolution suffered its final defeat.[5] Napoleon's had been the most ambitious attempt to create an empire in order to transform a nation, and the final effort prior to Hitler's Third Reich to establish an empire on European soil. Like the Third Reich, the Napoleonic empire did not last for long but at its height in 1812 it contained forty-four million subjects, about 40 per cent of the entire European population. It was also (unlike the Third Reich) to have a lasting influence on the future of the peoples of Europe. The British may have put an end to Napoleon but his vision of a united Europe would resurface in other less bellicose forms, and the European Union today possesses much in common with the declared objectives and political aspirations if not the cultural coerciveness of the Napoleonic dream.

France, however, was by no means the only European nation to employ the idea of empire to unite what was in reality a divided and potentially unstable people. Napoleon's arch-enemy Britain, monarchical and perfidious, employed very similar strategies. The viceregal pageantry with which Governor-General Lord Cornwallis celebrated his victory over Tipu Sultan of Mysore in 1792 combined images of Roman triumphalism with the transfigured image of 'imperial benevolence'. It was meant to enhance his own personal standing and to assure the peoples of India of the good intentions of the British. But it was also intended to enforce the concept of loyalty to the king in the face of the threat of working-class radicalism. Victoria's coronation as Empress of India in 1876 was the most fully-elaborated attempt the modern world has witnessed to recreate the ancient Roman *imperium*. Yet this, too, was meant for home consumption, a largely successful bid by the prime minister Benjamin Disraeli to enhance the faltering status of the monarchy. All such assertions of the power of the nation helped to press home both the legitimacy of its rulers and the strength of its identity. Even as late as 1902 the British coronation ceremony could be praised – in a sentence which ran together Burke's vision of an empire of liberty with nineteenth-century convictions of the racial superiority of the Anglo-Saxons – as the expression of the 'recognition, by a free democracy, of a hereditary crown as a symbol of the worldwide domination of their race'. In this way empire, as the historian Eric Hobsbawm has observed, 'made good ideological cement'.[6] The very existence of colonies could be a source of patriotic pride. 'The people who colonize the most,' wrote the French economist Paul Leroy-Beaulieu in 1874, 'is the first among all peoples.' 'C is for colonies' declared the *ABC for Baby Patriots* published in 1899, in a more belligerent mood:

> Rightly we boast,
> That of all the great nations
> Great Britain has the most.

In order to give the baby patriot a better understanding of what these colonies were and what their submissive inhabitants looked like, during the nineteenth century displays of 'natives' became a regular attraction in the imperial capitals of Europe. The Great Exhibition of 1851 brought to London peoples from every corner of the empire and exhibited them alongside the flora and fauna of their native habitat, so that Eskimos were placed alongside polar bears, and Africans with chimpanzees. As late as 1924–5, the Wembley Exhibition (also in London) included samples of what were tastefully described as 'peoples in residence'. These included Yoruba, Hausa and Fante Mende from West Africa, some Indians, and even 175 Chinese from Hong Kong. Most of them were set up in reconstructions of indigenous housing and could be seen working away at their local crafts and manufactures, the valuable commodities which would eventually flow home in one form or another to the metropolis.

Nor, of course, was the British empire the only one to relish such indirect glimpses of the exotic fringes of its domains. Eighteen 'colonial pavilions' complemented the newly-constructed Eiffel Tower in 1889, and the Paris exhibition of 1900 contained 'colonial villages' in which colourful native peoples could be seen from behind high wire fences going about their daily lives and staring back at those who had come to stare at them. The 1904 St Louis World Fair in Missouri became famous not only as the place where the ice-cream cone was first invented, but for the Philippine Exposition which contained a number of Filipino Villages exhibiting the various peoples of the archipelago, the 'savages' and 'Non Christian tribes', the Negritos and Igorots (whose nudity outraged the puritan sensibilities of the visitors – and attracted them in their thousands), as well as a large contingent of American-trained and dressed Filipino soldiers, there to demonstrate the possibilities for 'evolution' of even the most backward peoples under US colonial patronage.[7]

All of these exhibitions served a double role. They were part of the development of the new social sciences which, since the closing years of the eighteenth century, had begun to exercise a powerful influence not only on the imagination of the élites of Europe but also gradually on the ways in which empire was both conceived and administered. Just as Aotourou and Omai had been brought back as living evidence of the habits and customs of early humankind, so too were their descendants – only now they came in far larger numbers. They were also proof of the benefits which the European policies of 'civilizing' could have. The concept of 'civilizing', and 'civilization' had in one guise or another been an objective of all Europe's imperial ventures since Rome, and it relied upon widely-accepted notions of a universal human nature and law of human evolution. All peoples, it was believed, move from a condition of savagery through one of 'barbarism' until they finally reach the present civilized condition of the European. Along the way their means of production changes from hunting to pastoralism, agriculture and finally commerce; their forms of government evolve from tribalism, through despotism to monarchy; their beliefs grow from simple superstition to true religion and eventually, of course, into Christianity. In the course of their histories, they also put on clothes, acquire arts and sciences, learn how to write and preserve a record of their past, and finally start to build and live in cities.

The vast differences that separated the various peoples of the world could all be explained by a combination of factors. These included climate, terrain, modes of government, or time spent in migration. A people such as the Chinese might be held back for centuries by an inert and despotic mode of government. The American Indians had only developed the rudiments of a political culture because they had had to travel all the way from Mongolia across the Bering Strait to reach their present home. The 'primitive' condition of the Polynesians could be attributed to their isolation from the rest of humankind. However, because all peoples were basically the same, since the human race was a single species and the descendants of a single pair, all could in time acquire the features of civilization which, because of their good fortune, the Europeans had been the first to achieve. Just as the missionaries had assumed that all rational peoples would be able to understand the gospel once it had been explained to them, so the new apostles of civilization believed that the 'backward races' of the world, as they came to be called, were merely waiting for instruction. The peoples of America, Asia and Africa, enthused the marquis de Condorcet in 1793, 'seem to be waiting only to be civilized and to receive from us the means to be so, and find brothers among the Europeans to become their friends and disciples'.[8]

Condorcet's remarks reflect a revised conception of empire as a form of exchange which would come to dominate imperial ideologies in the nineteenth century. The white man's benefits were more than amply compensated for by what Rudyard

Kipling famously called 'the white man's burden'. They, the 'uncivilized', the 'savage', the 'barbarian' would give the Europeans their labour and their raw materials, their 'surplus' as it comfortingly came to be called; the Europeans in compensation would bring them enlightenment, technology, Christianity, even cleanliness. In one of the more curious advertisements for the joint virtues of empire and industry, the soap manufacturers Pears issued in 1887 a poster entitled 'The Formula of British Conquest'. It depicted a collection of semi-naked Sudanese, staring in wonder – one is even on his knees in an attitude of prayer – at a rock on which are written the words PEARS' SOAP IS THE BEST. Cleanliness is not only next to godliness. It is one of the defining marks of civilization. And the Europeans could be relied upon to provide it.

The notion that the European imperialists were the agents of progress, preparing those whom Kipling described as the 'new-caught sullen peoples, half devil and half child'[9] to assume one day their allotted place as masters of their own destiny, persisted until the twentieth century. It had been around in one form or another since antiquity. Aristotle had held similar views about the development of peoples and so, too, had Cicero. In its modern form however it was an Enlightenment notion which had been developed by essentially well-meaning cosmopolitans in the salons of Paris, London, Edinburgh and Berlin. It rested upon the overwhelming conviction that all human identity is shaped wholly and solely by the worlds which people inhabit. Even those early and sometimes radical distinctions which Christians had made between believers and non-believers never supposed a division within humankind itself. 'When we pray,' said the thirteenth-century mystic Ramon Llull, 'let us remember the pagans who are of our same blood.' 'Civilization', like Christianity, was a world open to all who chose to enter it.

In the early nineteenth century, however, a darker and more lasting way of understanding difference began to make an appearance: racism. Racism worked with a quite different set of assumptions from the historical evolutionism of the Enlightenment. It assumed that the human family was not one but many. It assumed that those different families were marked out by their appearance, their abilities and, in some quasi-religious sense, by the purposes for which they had been created. And it supposed that those differences, since they were as we would say today 'genetically determined', could not be altered substantially by education, persuasion or example. Some kind of racialism, and certainly implicit forms of racial discrimination, have been a feature of all human societies. But modern racism was different in being based on the new scientific cultures which grew up in Europe at the end of the eighteenth century and which were confident that ultimately everything about the human condition could be explained in terms of biology or physiology. It has always had many faces, and it has always included many and often contradictory theories. All, however, insist that distinctions between peoples are to be found not in culture but in nature, that some races have been granted superior qualities to others, and that racial features can only change by means of biological contact with other races.

In 1841 Jules Joseph Virey, a distinguished and much-respected physician, delivered a lecture to the Académie de médecine in Paris on the biological causes of civilization. Humanity was, he argued, divided into two groups: the 'whites', a term which included all Caucasians; and the 'blacks', who were the Africans, Americans and Asians. The 'whites', he told his audience, 'have attained a more or less perfect stage of civilization', while the 'blacks' struggle for survival in a 'constantly imperfect civilization'. Struggle as they might, the 'blacks' would always remain half-savage, imperfectly civilized. Their destiny was inscribed in the colour of their skin. The reason for this, Virey believed, was that the process of civilization in humankind is akin to that of domestication in animals. Domestic animals, such as cows, and civilized humans have white (or whitish) flesh; untamed animals, such as deer, and uncivilized humans have dark flesh. You only have to compare veal with venison. (Virey passed over in silence the fact that, as sixteenth-century anatomists had discovered, the flesh of all humans is the same colour. Only the skin differs.)

Having thus appropriated humans to the categories to be found in the animal world, Virey was able to draw the obvious conclusion that just as the wild animal was the natural prey of man so the 'black' human was the natural prey of the 'white'. Human beings might not kill and eat other human beings – which would nonetheless seem to be the logical conclusion to draw from his analogy – but it was natural for white humans to enslave black humans. Slavery might seem cruel and abhorrent but such were the ways of nature. 'Is it any more unjust,' he asked 'for the lion to devour the gazelle?' Racism such as Virey's – and it was fairly typical of the cruder range of arguments used both in Britain and in France particularly after the invasion of Algeria in 1830 – made of the Europeans a distinct and special category, especially gifted and ultimately destined to reduce all the other races to some kind of servitude. No one could now say, as a sixteenth-century Spanish Jesuit had once done, that an 'Ethiopian' brought up in Europe would be in all respects save for the colour of his skin a European.[10] Colour of skin and all that was believed to lie underneath it became the whole person.

On Virey's reckoning whites were superior because they were white. But their superiority also had a history. In the 1780s the orientalist Sir William Jones had developed the idea that certain linguistic affinities between Sanskrit and most of what are now called the Indo-European languages implied that all the peoples who spoke those languages must have had a common ancestry. These peoples, the European *Ur-Volk*, he called Aryans. Jones, who was an employee of the East India Company and ranked the sages of ancient India, Valmiki, Vyasa and Kalidasa, as equal to Plato and Pindar, believed that he had established an association between two great but otherwise distinct cultures. The link he had created between ancient Greece and ancient India was linguistic and not racial, but the implications of his belief that a common language supposed a common identity were taken up by later scholars. In particular, the German philologist Max Müller who became Professor of Sanskrit at Oxford in the 1860s and 1870s, developed Jones' ideas into a theory which provided the Aryans with a common racial heritage, a complex migratory history, and an ancestral home in southern Russia. From there they had supposedly spread out and colonized a vast area of land reaching all the way from northern India to western Europe, carrying with them that distinctive way of life, urban and law-governed, which by the late eighteenth century had come to be called 'civilized'. Müller's account became so widely accepted that by the time the

English jurist and Law Member of the Viceroy of India's Council, Henry Maine, came to write his immensely influential *Ancient Law* in 1861 he could declare categorically that civilization was 'nothing more than the name for the old order of the Aryan world'.[11]

At first, racism was limited to broad general distinctions between Europeans, Jews and Arabs, Africans, Chinese, and American Indians, peoples who were obviously distinct in appearance and habitat. Soon, however, as with the older languages of culture and 'national character', it came to be applied to different peoples within Europe itself. The self-styled Count Arthur de Gobineau, often referred to as the father of racist ideology, in *On the Inequality of the Human Races* (1853–5) tried to demonstrate that the Germans and the French aristocracy (whom he assumed to be pure 'Gothic' and thus of Germanic stock) had retained the original virtue of the Aryan peoples. All the rest, mongrelized and bastardized by centuries of interbreeding, had long since abandoned the civilized ways of their remote ancestors.[12]

Gobineau's work was based on a nostalgia for pre-revolutionary France and it had few followers except among backward-looking monarchists and some Germans (a Gobineau Society was founded in Germany in 1894). But by the middle of the nineteenth century a somewhat less extreme and rather less pessimistic racial curtain had been lowered across Europe which followed, roughly, the line of the confessional divide that emerged after the Reformation. In the north were what the liberal philosopher John Stuart Mill, who was also an employee of the East India Company, called the 'self-helping and struggling Anglo-Saxons', in the south the languid, potentially passive and generally despotic Latins – a group which, despite Mill's admiration for the great French philosopher and statesman Alexis de Tocqueville, also included the French.[13] The liberal parliamentarian Sir Charles Dilke in an account of his travels through the British empire, or what he called Greater Britain, remarked that although the Anglo-Saxon peoples were not the same everywhere – climate, environment and upbringing could still take their toll – 'essentially the race continues to be ours'. The future of the world, he claimed, belongs 'to the Anglo-Saxon, to the Russian and the Chinese races' – although the last, he observed, tended to fall under the 'influence of India and the Crown Colonies of Great Britain'. All the others would go to the wall or, like the Maoris, Australian Aborigines, 'Hottentots' and American Indians – those 'dying nations' singled out for extinction by Lord Salisbury in 1898 – vanish altogether.

Ultimately, however, all racial arguments ran into considerable difficulties. If the 'Aryans' were the originators of the peoples of India, Russia and Europe, this made the Indians and the British descendants of a common ancestor. The Indian, as one Indian civil servant observed, 'is like the Englishman, of an Ancient Aryan stock, a fellow subject of the Queen, and an industrious and law abiding citizen', which was why in the 1890s Lord Curzon's government had warned that Indians should on no account be placed in the same category as black Africans for the latter stood 'far below them' in what Curzon called 'the grades of humanity'. What, then, could possibly justify the British occupation of India or what the British saw as their self-evident superiority over its inhabitants? The only possible answer seemed to lie in what enlightened eighteenth-century theorists such as Diderot had eagerly endorsed and nineteenth-century ones most feared: miscegenation.

At some early stage in their history, it was claimed, the Aryan invaders of India had mingled with inferior aboriginal races who were grouped under the headings Dravidian (in southern India) and Turanian, a loose term embracing most non-Indo-European and non-Semitic language groups. Thereafter, racial interbreeding had weakened the Aryan strain until by the time the British arrived the amount of true Aryan blood that remained in some places was 'infinitesimally small'.[14] The view that interbreeding always resulted in the weakening of the supposedly stronger and superior stock was widely held and applied to Africa and America as well as to Asia. But no one could really explain why it did not work the other way round. Why had the Aryans not elevated the Dravidians and Turanians? After all horse-breeding, which provided the model for much racial theorizing, assumed the predominance of strength rather than weakness. If that were the case with horses, then why not with humans? Racists could never really find answers to such questions. Like the previous cycle of 'barbarism' and 'civilization', racism tended to assume that the hold of the superior peoples over the rest of the world was at best a tenuous one. There was a persistent dread among European colonists that, as Herder had foretold, it would be only a matter of time before the European civilizers and colonizers would themselves become 'natives' – either that or they would perish altogether.

Despite obvious problems of coherence, a belief in a common racial ancestry played a crucial role in the attempt of the British to rule India. Working on the assumption of a common Aryan heritage, they ransacked Sanskrit texts and questioned local religious leaders in an effort to discover a 'purer' form of Hinduism which would be closer to its unsullied Aryan sources and therefore more in keeping, or so they hoped, with their own notions of 'morality'. British India could then be governed in accordance with Hindu laws, or at least with those laws that could be made commensurable with English common law. 'I write and feel,' declared Lord Bentinck, governor-general of India between 1828 and 1835, 'as a legislator for the Hindus and as I believe many enlightened Hindus must feel.'

Bentinck's self-image as the restorer of the ancient Aryan law found its most dramatic expression in the struggle to outlaw sati (suttee), the custom whereby a widow would throw herself, or be pushed by relatives, onto the funeral pyre of her husband so as to perish with him. Sati challenged the concern of the British with 'improving' the Indians at the same time as it pandered to sexual fantasies and nightmares about the exotic Orient. For a society still addicted to public executions and in the process of becoming deeply perplexed about its own sexuality, sati combined sexual prurience with violence in a way that ensured it a great deal of public attention in Britain. Bentinck succeeded in outlawing the practice in 1829 not only on the grounds that it was inherently barbarous and a violation of 'natural justice' but because he had discovered that it was a later corruption of the original Sanskrit law. Its abolition was therefore 'a restorative act' which returned to the Indians their true culture.[15] When a statue of Bentinck by Richard Westmacott was erected in 1835 it showed him gazing into a morally improved future and standing on a drum around which, cast in bronze bas-relief, was a scene of impending sati. A young, remarkably European-looking woman with naked breasts, her sari slipping tantalizingly from her hips, her wailing children torn from her, is being dragged backwards onto the pyre by swarthy, turbaned male relatives. It is a typical piece of Victorian neoclassical eroticism, its images blending the ever-present threat of the (male) 'barbarian' with the feminized 'other' which haunted the overexcited minds of the guardians of the British Raj. Like the climate which rotted leather and turned fine cloth into fungus, and the all-too-potent Indian diseases, Indian sexuality – the writhing dancers of Lucknow, the many-armed goddess Kali – threatened to rot the stout British male from within; his body, in the steaming imagination of Lord Kitchener, commander-in-chief of the British army in India, risked being eaten away by 'slow cankerous and stinking ulcerations'.

The belief in a common ancestry for both Indians and Europeans also implied that beneath the trappings of later non-Aryan elements it might be possible to find in India customs, habits, even institutions that had all but vanished in Europe itself. One of these, which was largely the creation of Henry Maine, was the so-called 'village republic'. Maine persuaded himself that in the traditional, self-sufficient and to some degree self-governing Indian village he had discovered a living instance of what both the ancient Greek *polis* and the German or Scandinavian *mark* had once been. If he was right, then the village republic was an example of the kind of community from which the prevailing social order of the democratic nations of modern Europe had developed. As such, of course, it had to be protected and to some degree preserved.

In the long term, such images of continuity between the European past and the Indian present, and a wish to represent themselves as the more liberal heirs of the Mughal empire, meant that the British in India never attempted to effect very much long-term change in society. Not only did the village republics remain (as they remain to this day) largely unaltered, so too did the various local autocracies to which they belonged. For one of the things Maine seems to have overlooked was that whereas the *polis* and the *mark* had no ultimate overlords, the Indian villages did have. The Indian princely estates were untouched by the Raj and the princes themselves became, in effect, satraps of the British government in Westminster. As Jawaharlal Nehru remarked, it was ironic at least that the British, committed to the progressive amelioration of the Indian peoples into responsible democratic subjects of the crown, should have left so much intact of the backward, static monarchy they had overthrown.

In Africa also, where no notions of a common cultural heritage could apply, the British did their best to avoid much direct intervention in the prevailing social order. They ruled as far as possible through, rather than over, the colonized peoples. It was cheaper, likely to be less troublesome, and fitted well with British notions of empire as a species of paternal custodianship. From this there evolved the doctrine of 'indirect rule'. Here too, the imperial administration was aided by a complex intellectual and scientific (or pseudo-scientific) machine. Just as racialist notions about Aryanism and the studies of Indian culture by Jones and other orientalists had guided the British administration in India, so in Africa the imperial government at the beginning of the twentieth century was influenced by the new science of social anthropology.

As preliterate, preindustrial peoples, the African societies had to be spoken for, and the people who spoke for them were the anthropologists. Something which might be called anthropology had been around since at least the middle of the eighteenth century. But the modern, empirical social science based on extensive first-hand knowledge of the peoples being studied is a creation of the first decades of the twentieth century, and it was in part at least a creature of empire. The most successful and by far the most influential of the anthropologists in Britain (French anthropology was less involved in imperial affairs) were those who belonged to what has come to be called the 'functionalist' school, whose intellectual progenitor was the Polish émigré Bronislaw Malinowski. Malinowski believed that African societies were too fragile and fragmented to accept rapid or dramatic change – something which, in those areas where such changes were attempted, proved to be all too true. The role of the anthropologist was to instruct government in how to make the best of these delicate social worlds and to coax them into the European-dominated future without destroying them in the process. This, Malinowski believed, could only be achieved through understanding how they operated and by working as far as possible through native rulers. The hands-off administration of Africa which came to be called indirect rule was the creation of F. D. Lugard, governor and governor-general of Nigeria between 1912 and 1919, and was the product of long experience rather than anthropological reflection. But it was, Malinowski triumphantly declared, 'a complete surrender to the functional point of view'.

Indirect rule applied, however, only in north and central Africa where the economies were based largely on cash crops and where the climate made settlement unattractive. In southern Africa by contrast, in South Africa itself, Southern Rhodesia (Zimbabwe) and Kenya, the existence of rich arable lands and

ry of diamonds and precious metals attracted not
nt agents but private land-speculators and freebooters
il Rhodes. Here, for a while, they enjoyed a freedom of
manoeuvre which they could never have had in Asia. When the
men of Rhodes' Pioneer Column set out from the Cape Colony
in 1890 to occupy what was to become Southern Rhodesia they
behaved, leaving aside obvious differences in technology, much
as Cortés and Pizarro had done over 300 years before. They
seized African land and cattle as and when they chose or
required, brutally suppressing all opposition they met first from
the Ndebele in 1893-4 and then from the Ndebele and Shona in
1896-7. In southern Africa the lesson of America, even of India,
had finally been forgotten. The language of the 'empire of liberty'
had been silenced along with any notion of respect for the
fragility of the 'primitive'. The conquistador was back. But now
he was armed with a Gatling gun.

By the mid-1870s what has come to be called the 'scramble
for Africa' among the major, as well as a number of minor,
European powers had begun. By 1895 the French had an empire
in West Africa three times the size of the British, although
Britain managed to secure the major resources in terms of both
trade and population. The Germans occupied large areas of East
and South-West Africa. King Leopold of Belgium owned, as a
private individual since the Belgian parliament wanted nothing
to do with it, a region of nearly a million square miles in the
Congo Basin which in 1908 became the Belgian Congo. The
Italians had established a protectorate over the Indian Ocean
coastlands of Somalia; the Portuguese in Angola had transformed what had begun as a costal trading station into a full-
scale colony; and the Spanish still clung to Morocco and the

island of Fernando Po. By the outbreak of war in 1914 the entire continent – with the exception of a few isolated enclaves, the Republic of Liberia and the Empire of Ethiopia – was under the direct or indirect control of one or another European power.

The French, Dutch, Germans, Spanish, Belgians, Portuguese, Italians, and even briefly the Danes, all had at one time or another a stake in the African continent. But none of them except the Dutch had any significant imperial interests elsewhere in the world. By the second half of the nineteenth century, Britain was alone in having an empire that reached across the world and not only embraced a myriad different peoples and cultures but, while clinging to the ideals of representative government and liberty, included almost every possible kind of social and political community. It was a curious, hybrid beast. 'I know of no example of it either in ancient or modern history,' wrote Disraeli in 1878. 'No Caesar or Charlemagne ever presided over a dominion so peculiar.' It was multiracial and multireligious, diverse in manners and customs, united only in what he called the recognition of 'the commanding spirit of these islands'.[16]

Some kind of answer to Disraeli's puzzlement was provided in a book published in 1883 by the historian John Robert Seeley, called *The Expansion of England*, which rapidly became a bestseller. Seeley argued that the British empire had evolved as a new form of federalism. He did not invoke either Cicero or Cartwright, but his conception of what he now called 'imperialism' was markedly similar to theirs. The empire, as he understood it, was a world federation. His models were the United States which had expanded across a continent in the years after independence and created new, semi-autonomous states without changing either its political system or the allegiance of those states to the federal government, and to a lesser degree the federated states of the massive Russian empire. 'Federalism' for Seeley was yet another expression of what he saw as the genius of the 'Anglo-Saxon' peoples and, more widely, of Europeans in general. In his perhaps prophetic view, federations were destined sooner rather than later to replace what he called the 'country-states' which then dominated the Western world. 'Russia and the United States,' he wrote, 'will surpass in power the states now called great as much as the great country-states of the sixteenth century surpassed Florence.'[17] As Seeley saw it, Britain could either attempt to retain her status as a still-great 'country-state' and eventually, like Spain and Portugal, pass into national insignificance, or else transform herself and her empire from a metropolis surrounded by a number of divergent and distinct colonies into a federal superpower.[18] To do that, of course, she would have to grant a far greater measure of independence to those colonies than they currently enjoyed and that, Seeley recognized, as Adam Smith had done over a century earlier, no imperial power was ever likely to do. In many respects Seeley's vision of Britain's options has turned out to be remarkably precise. Except, of course, that as the 'country-state' now slowly loses its enduring pre-eminence, the form of federation that has arisen to replace it is not British but European.

Whatever its ultimate future, the British empire in the early twentieth century remained committed to the view that the justification for its survival was its mission to 'civilize' the 'barbarian' and in so doing to bring the peoples of the world together into a single worldwide community. Implicit in all this was the notion that one day, in however distant a future, the colonized peoples of the world would indeed become 'civilized'. When that happened, they would logically have to be given back control of their own lives. Lord Macaulay in his speech on the renewal in 1833 of the East India Company's charter had declared that 'by good government we may educate our subjects into a capacity for better government; that having become instructed in European knowledge they may, in some future age, demand European institutions'. He did not know when it would come but he declared that when it did 'it will be the proudest day in English history'.[19]

11 *Ending*

The rapid exploration of the Pacific and the settlement by the British in Australia and New Zealand had by the end of the eighteenth century extended the cordon of European influence and maritime power around the entire globe. The Europeans were now well on their way to establishing the hegemony which would survive until the middle of the twentieth century. Their only remaining competitors were China and the Ottoman empire. Although visibly failing even by the end of the eighteenth century, they were still powerful enough to command respect as independent powers well into the nineteenth. The Ottoman sultanate resisted European incursions by playing off one power against another in what came to be called the 'Great Game', and staggered on until the end of the nineteenth century. By 1900, however, little remained of the ancient sultanate and in 1908 it was seized by a group of liberal reformers known collectively as the Young Turks who attempted to transform it into a modern secular republic.[1]

China, although it was regarded as a valued and powerful trading partner, was already beginning to look vulnerable to rapacious English eyes when Lord George Macartney made his famous visit on behalf of the East India Company and George III in 1793. Macartney is best remembered today for his celebrated refusal to perform the traditional kowtow before the emperor.[2]

His defiance was not merely a question of personal honour. Ambassadors can be relied upon to set personal dignity aside when called upon to do so, and Macartney was a good ambassador. His refusal to grovel before the Son of Heaven was rather a measure of his conviction that what he looked upon as a suspicious, introverted civilization could not long resist the raw power of free trade – nor ultimately, although this still lay some distance in the future, the power of western technology. The Middle Kingdom was clearly a society which had grown ancient and moribund. It now stood, said Herder, 'as an old ruin on the verge of the World'.[3] One push and over it would go. And, of course, the innovative, unceremonial, individualistic Europeans were there to do the pushing.

Within a few years the Europeans, the British and French in particular, were making increasingly intemperate demands that the Chinese open their doors to 'foreign devils', demands which culminated in the so-called Opium Wars of 1839–42. Britain extended its base at Hong Kong and virtually detached Tibet which it considered to be properly a part of British India (thus creating a dispute over the status and sovereignty of the mountain kingdom which still rages today). In 1859 the British also established the Imperial Maritime Customs, a vast bureaucracy nominally under the control of the emperor but acting largely in British commercial interests. Germany set up bases in the north of the country while the French, who had already occupied Indonesia, extended their influence over the south.

In 1900, Britain, France, Russia, Italy, Germany, the USA and Japan (which had already seized Korea and Taiwan) joined forces to put down the so-called Boxer Rebellion and loot Beijing. In 1911, as a direct consequence of these incursions, the Chinese empire, which had survived since the days of Genghis Khan, collapsed before an internal rebellion which delivered it into the hands of a number of regional commanders known in the West as warlords under whose control it remained until the communist takeover in 1949. For both the West and the newly communist East, imperial China no longer represented (as it had done to so many in the eighteenth century when all things Chinese were in vogue) an example of enviable political stability as the only empire in the history of the world to have endured for centuries. It became instead an example of 'Oriental despotism', of all that was most damaging to the human spirit in the power of tradition, hierarchy, and veneration of the past.

The final demise of the mighty Chinese empire left the world in the hands of the major European powers, Russia and the United States. In the year 1800 they occupied or controlled some 35 per cent of the surface of the planet, by 1878 67 per cent, and by 1914 over 84 per cent.[4] Before long, however, as with all previous imperial orders, this virtual hegemony began to falter. By 1945, after two world wars, fought largely between Western powers for Western ends – 'Europe's two great civil wars', the Spanish statesman Salvador de Madariaga once called them – it was obviously nearing its end. The new European empires of the twentieth century, the would-be empires of Hitler and Mussolini, rose and fell in the space of a very few years. The empire which was the USSR, an extension to the west of the older empire of the tsars, fell with the ideology which had sustained it although it survives, fitful and divided, to the east. The European overseas empires all disappeared between 1947 and the late 1960s. Britain still has fourteen colonies, although they are now officially described as 'dependent territories' – and, more contentiously, continues to rule over the province of Northern Ireland. The Commonwealth lives on as a tattered coda to Burke's 'empire of liberty'. France has overseas provinces in the Pacific and the Indian Ocean. Spain still clings to Ceuta and Melilla on the North African coast. But these are mostly just fading memories.

The fall of the modern European empires was as rapid as their rise had been. And in most places the reasons for their downfall were similar. Ultimately, all had maintained their rule through acquiescence rather than by force or the threat of force. True, there had been some nasty episodes. But brutal and unwarranted as might have been, say, the suppression of the so-called Indian Mutiny of 1857, it failed in the long run to alter substantially the balance of power between the British and their Indian subjects. What had applied to the Roman empire also applied to the British, French, German and, ultimately, even the Russian empires: subject peoples were only willing to remain in sub-jection so long as at least a significant number of them could see some benefit in doing so. Furthermore, unlike any of the previous empires, those which had grown up after the beginning of the nineteenth century had rarely, except in southern Africa, exported many of their own peoples or created substantial creole élites capable of resisting native insurgency when it finally came.

Resistance to any kind of rule requires organization and courage. In the case of resistance to colonial rule, it also requires some vision of a better future in a postcolonial world. It requires an ideology capable of mobilizing those who might otherwise accept the status quo as inevitable. Ironically, this was provided by the same refashioning of society that had been the driving force behind most modern imperialism, namely nationalism. Of all Lord Macaulay's 'European institutions' the only one that most colonial peoples in the twentieth century have consistently demanded is the independent nation-state.

The imperial powers had provided indigenous élites with as much education as they saw fit in order to run the lower reaches of their empires for them. In so doing they had also armed them with modernizing ideals and Western notions of national self-determination. From Ireland to Java, the nation seemed to offer what has been called by the political scientist Benedict Anderson an 'imagined community' – a community which, although it has none of the properties that older face-to-face societies like the village or parish once offered, nevertheless holds out the prospect of belonging to a larger and potentially more powerful grouping.[5]

In most cases, if not all, such communities did not already exist. They had to be created. To achieve this it was widely believed that the territories they occupied had to correspond to the language and ethnic group of the majority of their inhabitants. In extreme cases those who spoke some other language or belonged to another ethnic group would have to be either deported or, if they would not or could not go, annihilated. Ethnic cleansing is by no means an invention of the post-Soviet world. Above all, of course, the nation had to be self-governing. The claim that national self-determination could only be achieved with full state independence – a belief to which Basque and Corsican extremists still cling – had emerged in the 1870s as an ideal during the struggle for national recognition within Europe itself as various nationalities, Italians, Germans, Irish and Polish, sought independence from the Austro-Hungarian, British and Russian empires. It was only a matter of time before the same ideals and expectations took root in Europe's overseas dependencies.

And when they did the consequences were devastating. Within a very brief space of time, from the end of the First World War until the mid-1960s, the nationalisms of the formerly dependent peoples had swept the once-massive imperial edifices away. In some places, the imperialists recognized that their time was up and got out while they could with some dignity and not too much expense. The British scuttled away from most of their possessions in Africa and the Caribbean, leaving behind them unstable island economies which have only been saved, if saved they have been, by the arrival of American tourism. Portuguese Goa was finally occupied by Indian troops in 1961. Hong Kong, the last British colony of any size, was handed back to China in 1997, with a ceremony like something out of Gilbert and Sullivan to mark the final going-down of the British sun. In contrast, Macao, the last Portuguese factory in Asia, went two years later almost without anyone noticing. In others places – the Belgian Congo, Algeria, Cyprus, Rhodesia (seized by its white settler population in 1965), Angola, Mozambique – the departure was brutal and protracted. Colonial wars, wars of independence, wars by peoples to regain their status as peoples, were a constant feature of the first sixty or seventy years of the twentieth century and the hostilities they have created are likely to survive well into the first half of the twenty-first.

The processes of decolonization have left in their wake not only bitter memories and undying enmities. They have also created what sometimes appear to be insuperable dilemmas for the world's new nations. For not only is the nation a relatively new and entirely European conception, it is also the case that few of the former imperial districts from which most post-colonial nations have been constructed had any existence prior to the arrival of the Europeans. This was also true in the ancient world. Spain, Britain and Gaul were all in various ways creations of Rome. So, too, was Italy itself. Spanish vice-regal divisions lie behind the modern frontiers of the republics of Spanish America. The modern states of Eastern and Central Europe took shape under the aegis of the Holy Roman empire, and their present distribution of peoples is in large part the creation of the Austro-Hungarian empire, the empire of the Tsars, or the Soviet Union.

Nowhere is this effect as marked, and nowhere have its consequences been as far-reaching, as in the European empires in Asia and Africa. Here imperial foundations brought together peoples who shared very little with one another. Sometimes this was done simply by drawing boundary lines around the territories of a number of different and even hostile groups, sometimes through either forced or voluntary migration. This is most tragically obvious in Africa. Africa, as its postcolonial history has demonstrated all too brutally, is a land violated not just by the activities of European freebooters but by a false conception of ethnicity. Unlike India or much of Asia, or even ancient Mexico and Peru, sub-Saharan Africa before the arrival of the Europeans had very few very large-scale societies. One of the tragic consequences of indirect rule (for which the anthropologists cannot be held responsible) was the assumption that Africans were divided into what, in honour of some supposed affinity with early European societies, were called tribes. Most of these were either too large or too small to capture the complex ethnic divisions of most parts of the continent. The Bangala of Zaire, the Baluyia and Kikuyu of Kenya, the Bagisu of Uganda, and the Yoruba and Ibo of Nigeria were all colonial inventions. The Ibo were a New World fiction created by lumping together into a single ethnic and hence tribal group all slaves speaking any one of the (numerous) Ibo dialects. Such categorizations made the district officer's task easier. But as the division between the administrative areas of British, French, Belgian and German Africa hardened, they in their turn became the boundary lines of the new post-independence African states. The long-term consequences of this process proved to be disastrous. Ethnic divisions and conflict which could never have existed before the coming of the Europeans rapidly became, and have remained, the dominant feature of the continent.

Nearly all the modern postcolonial states have been in this way the creations of former imperial administrations. Today schoolchildren from Bulawayo still gather at the tomb of Cecil Rhodes in the Matopos Hills in south-eastern Zimbabwe just as they did when their country was Rhodesia. They do so not because their teachers and parents have any fond memories of British rule but because without Rhodes there would have been no modern nation for them to inherit.[6] Attempts to associate modern Zimbabwe in anything but name with the Munhumatapa empire which flourished in the high veldt in the sixteenth century remain unpersuasive as a national foundation. Although the historical connection is an obvious source of pride, as are the great ruins of Zimbabwe itself, modern Zimbabwe is the nation that Rhodes created and President Mugabe has inherited.

Inevitably, colonial peoples have also discovered that anti-colonialism and collective identity are not the same thing. It was much easier for Tamils, Brahmins, Bengalis, Sikhs, Malays, Nilotes or Ashantis to recognize that they were not Englishmen than it was for them to imagine themselves to be Singhalese, Indians, Pakistanis, Malayasians, Sudanese or Ghanaians.[7] In the early nineteenth century the 'liberator' of Peru, San Martín, in an effort to create a modern Peruvian nation which would incorporate both the white creole population and the former subjects of the Inca empire, issued an edict 'baptizing' all Quechua-speaking Indians as Peruvians. At one time or another all nationalists have had recourse to similarly desperate measures. And every nationalist has had good cause to echo the remark supposedly made by Ferdinando Martino, Italian minister of public instruction, in 1896, 'We have made Italy, now we must make the Italians.'[8]

Making Italians, or Indians or Cypriots or Malaysians, has often proved to be an impossible task. Once the imperial regime has been shaken off, once the new nation has been called into existence, complete with a collective identity marked by flags, national anthem, currency and postage, once a political élite has emerged or has been hastily assembled, once the imperialists and the settlers who still have somewhere to go have gone 'home' – then the old divisions which the empire had stifled and new ones which it had inevitably and sometimes intentionally created have further split the 'new' nations into ever smaller national and ethnic groupings. India, Pakistan, Nigeria, Cyprus, Indonesia, Malaysia have all since the end of British rule divided and subdivided. The same has been true of Vietnam, much of Central Africa after the expulsion of the French, and parts of

West Africa following the departure of the Portuguese. New nations can be brought into being with the flourish of a pen. New peoples take far longer to gestate.

Nor are former colonies the only states to experience this process. In Europe itself, processes that began on the edges of the empire at the end of the eighteenth century have in the twenty-first crept back to transform the metropolis itself, just as in their different ways Montesquieu and Tocqueville warned that they would. Spain, which the ministers of Philip III and IV in the seventeenth century, the enlightened monarch Charles III in the eighteenth, the liberals in the nineteenth and then, with savage ferocity, General Franco in the twentieth, all tried to fuse together out of Catalans, Basques, Castilians, Adalusians, Galicians, has now all but fallen apart. It is ruled over by a monarch who holds power in the name of the nation but, as he himself has said, that nation has in a little over twenty years become the first federal state of the new federal Europe. Even the United Kingdom, which although only united since the beginning of the eighteenth century seemed nevertheless to have been stable for far longer than any other European nation, is inexorably dissolving back into its component parts. 'Internal decolonization' it has been called, and there is no knowing where it will stop, no knowing what in the future might be the ideal unit that we choose to call a 'people'.

Creoles, indigenes and local separatists are not the only groups to make demands on the steadily dissolving body of empire. In a world in which the West no longer clings quite so self-confidently to its belief in the superiority of its way of life, in which attitudes towards the developing world in general have become far more ambiguous, the remaining aboriginal peoples of the world, in the Americas, Australia and New Zealand, have begun to insist on some measure of recognition. Creole states, from Argentina (which until thirty years ago denied the existence of any significant preconquest groups) to Canada, have modified their constitutions and re-examined original treaties of settlement.

Perhaps the most celebrated attempt by an indigenous group to reclaim its territory and its right to historical recognition is what has come to be called the 'Mabo Case'. In 1982, three representatives of the Meriam peoples living in the Murray Islands in the Torres Straits, Eddie Mabo, David Passi and James Rice, brought an action in the Australian High Court against the State of Queensland, claiming that 'the Meriam people were entitled to the Islands as owners, possessors, occupiers and as persons entitled to enjoy the Islands', and that 'the Islands were not and never had been "Crown Land"'. In order to make their case, they went on to argue that the claim made in 1788, whereby Australia had been declared to be *terra nullius* – 'unoccupied land' – and could thus be seized by anyone who chose to, had been invalid. In 1992, the Australian High Court ruled in their favour, thus depriving the Commonwealth of Australia of its sovereignty not merely over the Murray Islands but, by implication, over the entire continent. This was followed in December 1993 by the Native Title Act which, although it stopped short of handing back Australia to its aboriginal inhabitants, did set up measures to redress what the judges of the High Court called 'the national legacy of unutterable shame' which was, in their view, the history of the dealing of European settlers with the Aboriginals.

For many it has been a cathartic experience, a forced recognition that the creole nations that have evolved out of the
disappearance of the old European empires have never been one
and united. So far, few indigenous peoples have attempted full
autonomy from the nations by which they are encompassed.
(The Inuit nation created in northern Canada in 1999 is, despite
the ceremony with which it was inaugurated and the claims it
has made for itself, little more than a self-administered
province.) All aboriginal peoples are inescapably peoples of two
worlds. They are Mi'Kmaq and Canadian, Maori and New Zea-
lander. They share two cultures and may, as has happened on a
number of occasions, claim protection from one culture under
the laws of the other. No one resists the idea that cultures are
porous and subject to periodic reinvention so fiercely as the
spokespersons of aboriginal peoples. This is hardly surprising
since so much of their claim depends upon an appeal to continuing cultural difference. Yet few cultures are as poly-
morphous as they are. Everywhere in the world they nestle
within other cultures, predominantly of European origin, where
they constitute the minority. You cannot shed hundreds of
years of frequently oppressive and subservient coexistence by
nostalgia alone.

The difficulties faced by aboriginal peoples are, paradoxically,
not unlike those shared by other groups which, rather than
attempting to survive in their former homelands, have fled to
the metropolises of the empires by which they had once been
occupied. Whereas European settlers once flowed out to
America, Africa and Asia, Asians, Africans and the peoples of
the Caribbean are in increasing numbers flowing back to Europe.
These are not, as they are so often represented, isolated immi-

grant groups. They are full-scale migrations, peoples on the move, of a kind that Europe has not experienced since the final days of the Roman empire. Large communities have grown up which are in some cases very nearly autonomous – Bradford, in England, the Barbès district of Paris, and Chinatowns just about anywhere – and cling fiercely to the lifeways, cultural habits, beliefs, not to mention dress, languages and food of their original homelands. Yet even within these enclaves cultures cannot remain self-contained for long. The first generation may attempt as far as it is able to insulate itself from the surrounding, alien world. But the next generally want something more. While still recognizing themselves to be Pakistani or Algerian or Moroccan, they also and perhaps most clearly see themselves as British or French or Spanish. In most of the former European imperial capitals from London to Lisbon intermingling and intermarriage have gone a long way towards creating truly multiethnic communities. The frontier and the metropolis are no longer as distinct as they once were, and in the future the differences are likely to diminish even further.

While the memories of empire fade or are transformed at least within Europe itself, the idea of the nation, which had done so much, if only as an aspiration, to bring about their demise, is itself under threat. In recent years there has been much talk of globalization and the end of the nation-state. To most observers, however, it must seem that the nation-state still has a lot of life left in it. Peoples think of themselves overwhelmingly in nationalist terms. Those who do not are generally, as they have always been, the wealthy, the privileged, the intellectual. Diderot could afford to tell David Hume in 1768, 'You belong to all the nations of the earth and you never ask a man for his place of birth. I flatter myself that I am like you, a citizen of the great city of the world,' because while Diderot knew that he was also French and Hume knew himself to be what he called a 'North Briton' both of them also belonged to a cosy, self-sustaining universe which in their day was called 'the republic of letters' – a fictional, transcendental nation of the mind.[9] Today, the equivalent sentiments are more likely to be expressed by those who sit at the front in aeroplanes, international bankers and their friends, than among the intelligentsia. Cosmopolitanism has generally been a luxury that only aristocracies of one kind or another can really afford.

Yet for all the persistence of national sentiments there are signs that, as peoples once formed themselves into empires and thence into nations, they are in some parts of the world becoming peoples again. The European Union, which to so many of its enemies looks like an empire, is one arena in which the nation-state is being slowly and sometimes painfully transformed into a confederation. For all the problems it has encountered, it has demonstrated that sovereignty and cultural identity do not need to be inseparable and that it is possible to live by laws drafted by a multinational executive while remaining culturally tied just as firmly as before to local and national allegiances. More significantly perhaps, Europe is rapidly becoming an arena where being French, for instance, is no longer such a mystery to those who are British, or vice versa – where different cultural lives complement one another whereas before they were only a source of conflict. The outbursts of bloody chauvinism unleashed upon Eastern Europe after the collapse of the Soviet Union, and the European Union's apparent powerlessness in the face of them, might be taken as a depressing indication that what Sigmund Freud so tellingly called 'the narcissism of small differences' is still an enduring human passion. But for all that, as new generations of peoples grow up who are willing to think of themselves as Europeans, as well as German or Dutch or Portuguese, it is still possible to hope that nationalism as the expression of solidarity formed through the hatred of difference is steadily if slowly in retreat.

These changes, and it is impossible to say how far and how fast they will reach, have all occurred in a rapidly changing world, a world that has become 'global'. On closer examination, if we ignore the omnipresent fast-food chains and video games which are to be found across the planet from Belfast to Beijing, globalization turns out to be relatively restricted. It is a term applied more to economies than to culture or politics and, as the World Bank recently pointed out, the world economy is less unified today than it was a hundred years ago. Globalization has, however, become a scare-word which for many describes a vaster and infinitely more menacing universal empire than any of those that have preceded it.[10] Empires are no more, the argument goes, but the habits and customs which sustained those of Europe for so long are now being smuggled back in with markets, international funding agencies and well-meaning but generally misguided non-governmental organizations taking the place of armies, administrators and priests.

In one sense, this is historically misleading. Volkswagen, the World Bank, the IMF or the World Wide Fund for Nature are not easily identifiable as 'imperialist' even if the language they use and the behaviour of their employees frequently are. They do not serve a central state and their long-term objectives are only incidentally political. Yet it is clearly true, as the peoples of the developing world have protested so often and so bitterly, that the legacies of the older empires have not entirely gone away. The surrender of colonies, the undoing of institutions, even the abandonment of an enduring ideology do not always lead to the renunciation of a creed, a conviction, a way of life.

There remains an assumption that has been with us since the days of Alexander the Great that certain values, the values 'we' treasure, are not merely the expression of our desires and preferences but are in some larger sense the obvious and necessary values of humankind. Above all, the modern heirs of Alexander tend to assume that a rule of law which respects individual rights and liberal democratic government (as practised in the United States) is a universal and not, as it most surely is, the creation of Graeco-Roman christendom. In 1995 the United Nations published a document called *Our Global Neighbourhood*. Its authors set out to explain that although international law – the 'law of nations' – was historically 'made in Europe by European jurists to serve European ends' and was 'based on Christian values and designed to advance Western expansion', it nevertheless came up with the right answers because despite its origins it was responsible for the creation of a universal conception of the person. Therefore, they insist, 'no longer is it credible for a state to turn its back on international law, alleging a bias towards European values and influence'. All that humankind now requires, they conclude, in order to bring about that elusive but eternal dream of 'perpetual peace' is a 'global citizenship' based on 'a strong commitment to principles of equity and democracy grounded in civil society'.[11]

It is not hard to see beneath this, well-intentioned though it evidently is, something very similar to the Roman notion of the *civitas*. The law of nations – or, as one American political philosopher, John Rawls, has tried to redefine it, the 'law of peoples' – remains, just as it was for the Roman emperor Caracalla, a universal creed.[12] It may well be that as we move forward into the new millennium and better and faster systems of communication shrink our world we do require some common code that will be able to unite us all, if only at times of crisis. At present there seems to be none on offer other than the law of nations. We would do well, however, to remember in our multicultural enthusiasm that this, like all forms of universalism, was once created in order to make a group of peoples into an empire.

Droctulft's journey with which this book began – and the journeys of all the world's Droctulfts – is nearing its end. Byzantium is no more and Ravenna has become an industrial nightmare linked to a seedy seaside resort. Although he could hardly have guessed that it would turn out this way, the 'civilization' for which Droctulft abandoned one life and sacrificed another has now reached, almost, into the furthermost recesses of the world. The Englishwoman, the 'captive' to whom Borges' grandmother had spoken that evening on the Pampas a little over a century ago, has become, along with the peoples who seized her as an infant, a relic, a figure from an infinitely remote past. 'Barbarism' exists as truly as it ever did but it no longer has a home. Now we do not struggle, as Droctulft did, with invaders. We struggle only with ourselves.

Notes

INTRODUCTION

1 *De Consulatu Stilichonis*, III, 135–70.

2 Review of Herder's *'Ideas on the Philosophy of the History of Mankind'*, in *Kant: Political Writings*, ed. Hans Reiss (Cambridge, 1991), p. 220.

3 *Corpus Hermeticum*, ed. A. J. Festugière and Arthur Darby Knock (Paris, 1954), IV Fr. 23, pp. 14–16.

4 See the essays in Maurice Duverger (ed.), *Le concept d'empire* (Paris, 1980).

5 J. S. Richardson, *'Imperium Romanum*: Empire and the Language of Power', *Journal of Roman Studies*, LXXXI (1991), 1–9.

6 See Hugh Tinker, *A New System of Slavery: The Export of Indian Labour Overseas 1830–1920* (London, 1974).

7 Sunil Khilnani, *The Idea of India* (New York, 1997), p. 118.

8 *Novum Organum*, in *The Works of Francis Bacon*, ed. James Spedding, R. L. Ellis and D. D. Heath (London, 1857–74), IV, p. 92.

I. THE FIRST WORLD CONQUEROR

1 François Hartogh, *Mémoires d'Ulysse: Récits sur la frontière en Grèce ancienne* (Paris, 1996), pp. 12–13.

2 John Boardman, *The Greeks Overseas: Their Early Colonies and Trade* (New York and London, 1980).

3 Bartolomé de Las Casas, *A Short Account of the Destruction of the Indies*, trans. Nigel Griffin (London and New York, 1992), p. 15.

4 *The Fortunes of Alexander*, 327 ff.

5 Inga Clendinnen, ' "Fierce and Unnatural Cruelty": Cortés and the Conquest of Mexico', in *New World Encounters*, ed. Stephen Green-

blatt (Berkeley, Los Angeles and London, 1993), pp. 12–47.

6 Jared Diamond, *Guns, Germs, and Steel: The Fate of Human Societies* (New York and London, 1999), pp. 67–81.

7 The best modern account of Alexander's life and campaigns is A. B. Bosworth, *Conquest and Empire: The Reign of Alexander the Great* (Cambridge, 1988).

8 *Florida*, VII.

9 Ibid.

10 Plutarch, *Parallel Lives*, 'Pompey', 2.2; and Sallust, *Historiae*, 3.88 M.

11 Quoted by Robin Lane Fox, *The Search for Alexander* (Boston, 1980), p. 23.

12 *The Fortunes of Alexander*, 328b.

13 *Politics*, 1252 b 4.

14 *The Fortunes of Alexander*, 328b.

15 *Quaestiones naturales* VI, 23, and *Epistolae* 91.17.

16 The standard work is George Cary, *The Medieval Alexander* (Cambridge, 1956).

17 *The 'Alexandreis' of Walter of Châtillon: A Twelfth-Century Epic*, trans. David Townsend (Philadelphia, 1996), Book X.

2. THE EMPIRE OF THE ROMAN PEOPLE

1 The story is told by Aulus Gellius, *Noctes Atticae*, iv, 8.

2 D. O. Thomas (ed.), *Richard Price: Political Writings* (Cambridge, 1991), p. 38.

3 See Andrew Lintott, *Imperium Romanum: Politics and Administration* (London and New York, 1993).

4 *De Officiis*, 1.38.

5 *The Reason of State* [*Della ragion di stato*], trans. P. J. and D. P. Waley (London, 1956), pp. 6–7.

6 Quoted in P. A. Garney, 'Laus Imperii', in *Imperialism in the Ancient World*, ed. P. A. Garney and C. R. Whittaker (Cambridge, 1978), p. 168.

7 *De Legibus*, I, x, 29; xii, 33.

8 *Institutes*, Proemium.

9 S. Albert, *Bellum Iustum*, Frankfurter Althistorische Studien, 10 (Kallmunz, 1980).

10 *De Officiis*, 1.34–5: 'There are two types of conflict: the one proceeds by debate, the other by force. Since the former is the proper concern of man, but the latter of beasts, one should only resort to the latter if one may not employ the former.'

11 *De Republica*, 3.34.

12 *De Legibus*, 1. xxii. 4.

13 'Lectures on Law: Citizens and Aliens', in *The Works of James Wilson*, ed. Robert Green McCloskey (Cambridge, Mass., 1967) II, p. 581.

14 *Discorsi*, II, 2.

15 *De Officiis*, 2.27.

16 *De Otio*, 4.1.

17 Burton Stein, 'Vijayanagara', in *The New Cambridge History of India* (Cambridge, 1989), I, 2.

18 *De Consulatu Stilichonis*, III, 135–70. St Augustine's comment on Honorius is quoted by Peter Brown, *Augustine of Hippo: A Biography* (London, 1976), p. 291. See Richard Koebner, *Empire* (Cambridge, 1961), pp. 14–19.

19 Ernest Barker, 'The Conception of Empire', in *The Legacy of Rome*, ed. Cyril Bailey (Oxford, 1923), p. 53.

20 *De Republica*, VI, 19–20.

21 *Ab urbe condita libri*, XXXVIII, 60.5.

22 Claude Nicolet, *L'Inventaire du monde: géographie et politique aux origines de l'empire romain* (Paris, 1988).

23 This point is made by Mark Elvin, *The Pattern of the Chinese Past: A Social and Economic Interpretation* (Stanford, Ca., 1973), pp. 18–22.

24 *Ab urbe condita libri*, XXXVII, 35.

25 Henry Chadwick, 'Envoi: On Taking Leave of Antiquity', in *The Oxford History of the Classical World*, ed. John Boardman, Jasper Griffin and Oswyn Murray (Oxford and New York, 1986), p. 808.

26 Ramsay MacMullen, *Christianizing the Roman Empire A.D. 100–400* (New Haven and London, 1984).

27 For a general history of the empire see Michael Grant, *Historical Rome* (Englewood Cliffs, N.J., 1978).

3. UNIVERSAL EMPIRE

1 Marie Tanner, *The Last Descendant of Aeneas: The Habsburgs and the Mythic Image of the Emperor* (New Haven and London, 1993).

2 *Historia imperial y caesarea, en la qual en summa se contiene las vidas y hechos de todos los caesares imperadores de Roma desde Julio Caesar hasta el Emperador Carlos Quinto* (Antwerp, 1561), sig. I^v.

3 C. A. Bayly, *Imperial Meridian: The British Empire and the World 1780–1830* (Harlow, 1989), pp. 19–34.

4. CONQUERING THE OCEAN

1 For an authoritative account of Henry's life see Peter Russell, *Prince Henry 'The Navigator': A Life* (New Haven and London, 2000).

2 See Sanjay Subrahmanyam, *The Career and Legend of Vasco da Gama* (Cambridge, 1997).

3 On Columbus' life see Felipe Fernández Armesto, *Columbus* (New York and London, 1991).

4 *An Inquiry into the Nature and Causes of the Wealth of Nations*, ed. R. H. Campbell and A. S. Skinner (Oxford, 1976), p. 560.

5. SPREADING THE WORD

1 *De Civitate Dei*, V, 15.

2 Colossians, 11.

3 *Histoire d'un voyage faict en la terre du Bresil autrement dite Amerique* (Geneva, 1578).

4 The story is told, at length, by Bartolomé de Las Casas, *Historia de las Indias*, ed. Augustín Millares Carlo (Mexico and Buenos Aires, 1951), II, pp. 441–4.

5 *A Short Account of the Destruction of the Indies*, trans. Nigel Griffin (London and New York, 1992).

6 See Anthony Pagden, *The Fall of Natural Man: The American Indian and the Origins of Comparative Ethnology* (Cambridge, 1982), pp. 109–45.

7 *Boswell's Life of Johnson*, ed. G. B. Hill (Oxford, 1934), I, 45.

8 Quoted in *A Short Account of the Destruction of the Indies*, p. xiv.

6. THE DECLINE OF THE IBERIAN WORLD

1 Geoffrey Parker, 'David or Goliath? Philip II and His World in the 1580s', in *Spain, Europe and the Atlantic World: Essays in Honour of John H. Elliott*, ed. Richard Kagan and Geoffrey Parker (Cambridge, 1995), pp. 254–5.

2 See J. H. Elliott, *Spain and its World 1500–1700* (New Haven and London, 1989), pp. 241–62.

3 *An Inquiry into the Nature and Causes of the Wealth of Nations*, ed. R. H. Campbell and A. S. Skinner (Oxford, 1976), p. 563.

4 The best account of the Portuguese empire is A. J. R. Russell-Wood, *The Portuguese Empire, 1415–1808: A World on the Move* (Baltimore and London, 1992).

7. EMPIRES OF LIBERTY, EMPIRES OF TRADE

1 H. P. Biggar, *A Collection of Documents Relating to Jacques Cartier and the Sieur de Roberval*, Publications of the Public Archives of Canada, No. 14 (Ottawa, 1930), p. 128.

2 Stephen Greenblatt, *Marvellous Possessions: The Wonder of the New World* (Oxford, 1991), pp. 109–18.

3 *Judicious and Select Essays and Observations* (London, 1667), p. 20.

4 Anthony Pagden, *Lords of All the World: Ideologies of Empire in Spain, Britain and France, c. 1500–c. 1800* (New Haven and London, 1995), pp. 178–200.

5 Quoted in Steven Pincus, 'The English Debate over Universal Monarchy', in *A Union for Empire: Political Thought and the British Union of 1707*, ed. John Robertson (Cambridge, 1995), p. 42.

6 'A Discourse on Government with Relation to Militias', in *The Political Works of Andrew Fletcher* (London, 1737), p. 66.

7 James Axtell, *The Invasion Within: The Contest of Cultures in Colonial North America* (New York and Oxford, 1985), p. 133.

8 'Philo-Caledon', *A Defence of the Scots Settlement in Darien with an Answer to the Spanish Memorial against it* (Edinburgh, 1699), p. 24.

9 See Richard White, *The Middle Ground: Indians, Empires and Republics in the Great Lakes Region 1650–1815* (Cambridge, 1991).

10 *Speech of Edmund Burke Esq. on Moving his Resolution for Conciliation with the Colonies* (London, 1775), p. 48.

11 *An Inquiry into the Nature and Causes of the Wealth of Nations*, ed. R. H. Campbell and A. S. Skinner (Oxford, 1976), p. 61.

12 *The Writings and Speeches of Edmund Burke*, ed. Paul Langford (Oxford, 1981), II, p. 194.

13 David Armitage, 'The British Conception of Empire in the Eighteenth Century', in *Imperium/Empire/Reich: Ein Konzept politischer Herrschaft im deutsch-britischen Vergleich*, ed. Franz Bosbach and Hermann Hiery (Munich, 1999), pp. 91–107.

14 See in particular, P. J. Marshall, 'The British in Asia: Trade to Dominion, 1700–1765', in *The Oxford History of the British Empire*, Vol. II, *The Eighteenth Century*, ed. P. J. Marshall (Oxford, 1998), pp. 487–507.

15 Quoted in Rajat Kanta Ray, 'Indian Society and the Establishment of British Supremacy, 1765–1818', in ibid., p. 514.

16 *Political Writings*, ed. D. O. Thomas (Cambridge, 1991), p. 71.

17 *The Speeches of the Right Hon. Edmund Burke*, Vol. V, 'India, Madras and Bengal, 1774–1785', ed. P. J. Marshall (Oxford, 1981), p. 385.

18 See P. J. Marshall, *The Impeachment of Warren Hastings* (Oxford, 1965).

19 David Bromwich (ed.), *On Empire, Liberty and Reform: Speeches and Letters of Edmund Burke* (New Haven and London, 2000), pp. 15–16.

8. SLAVERY

1 See M. I. Finley ed. *Classical Slavery* (London and Totowa, N.J., 1987) and *Ancient Slavery and Modern Ideology* (New York, 1980).

2 Gomes Eanes de Zurara, *Crónica dos feitos na conquista de Guiné*, ed. Torquato de Sousa Soares (Lisbon, 1961), I, pp. 145–8.

3 See Robin Blackburn, *The Making of New World Slavery: From the Baroque to the Modern 1492–1800* (London, 1997).

4 Quoted in Anthony Pagden, *Lords of All the World: Ideologies of Empire in Spain, Britain and France, c. 1500–c. 1800* (New Haven and London, 1995), p. 171.

5 See Philip Curtin, *The African Slave Trade: A Census* (Madison, 1969).

6 *Politics*, 1254 b 27ff.

7 See Anthony Pagden, *The Fall of Natural Man: The American Indian and the Origins of Comparative Ethnology* (Cambridge, 1982), pp. 27–56.

8 Letter to Fray Bernardo de Vique O.P., in *Political Writings*, ed. Anthony Pagden and Jeremy Lawrance (Cambridge, 1991), pp. 334–5.

9 See David Eltis, *Economic Growth and the Ending of the Atlantic Slave Trade* (New York and London, 1987).

10 J. D. Farge, *A History of Africa* (London, Melbourne, Auckland and Johannesburg, 1978), pp. 339–40.

11 See Robin Blackburn, *The Overthrow of Colonial Slavery 1776–1848* (London and New York, 1998).

12 Quoted in Hugh Thomas, *The Slave Trade: The Story of the Atlantic Slave Trade: 1440–1870* (New York, 1997), pp. 789.

9. THE FINAL FRONTIER

1 Louis-Antoine de Bougainville, *Voyage autour du monde par la frégate la Boudeuse et la flûte l'Etoile; en 1766, 1767, 1768 and 1769* (Paris, 1980), pp. 133–70.

2 Bernard Smith, *European Vision and the South Pacific* (New Haven and London, 1985), p. 130.

3 *Histoire des navigations aux terres australes* (Paris, 1756), I, pp. 17–19.

4 *The Journals of Captain James Cook on his Voyages of Discovery*, ed. J. C. Beaglehole (Cambridge, 1955–67), Vol. I, 'The Voyage of the *Endeavour*, 1768–1771', p. 514.

5 Ibid., pp. cclxxx–cclxxxiii.

6 *European Vision and the South Pacific*, pp. 114–15.

7 *The Journals of Captain James Cook on his Voyages of Discovery*, Vol. III, 'The Voyage of the *Resolution* and *Discovery*, 1776–1779', pp. 239–59.

8 Bernard Smith, *Imagining the Pacific: In the Wake of the Cook Voyages* (New Haven and London, 1992), pp. 225–40.

10. EMPIRE, RACE AND NATION

1 *Outlines of a Philosophy of the History of Man* [*Ideen zur Philosophie der Geschichte der Menschheit*], trans. T. Churchill (London, 1800), p. 224.

2 See Anthony Pagden, *European Encounters with the New World: From Renaissance to Romanticism* (New Haven and London, 1993), pp. 172–9.

3 Richard Koebner, *Empire* (Cambridge, 1961), p. 277.

4 Edward Said, *Orientalism* (New York and London, 1979), pp. 81–5.

5 Henry Laurens, Charles C. Gillispie, Jean-Claude Golvin and Claude Traunecker, *L'Expédition d'Egypte: 1798–1801* (Paris, 1989).

6 *The Age of Empire, 1875–1914* (London, 1987), p. 70.

7 Paul Kramer, 'Making Concessions: Race and Empire Revisited at the Philippine Exposition, St Louis, 1901–1905', *Radical History Review*, 73 (1999), pp. 75–114.

8 *Esquisse d'un tableau historique des progress de l'esprit humain* (Paris, 1793), pp. 335–7.

9 *A Choice of Kipling's Verse, Selected with an Essay on Rudyard Kipling by T. S. Eliot* (London, 1963), p. 136.

10 On Virey see Anthony Pagden, 'The "Defence of Civilization" in Eighteenth-Century Social Theory', *History of the Human Sciences*, 1 (1988), pp. 33–45.

11 See, in general, Leon Poliakov, *The Aryan Myth: A History of Racist and Nationalist Ideas in Europe*, trans. E. Howard (London, 1974).

12 John Burrow, *The Crisis of Reason: European Thought, 1848–1914* (New Haven and London, 2000), pp. 106–7.

13 *Utilitarianism, Liberty, Representative Government*, ed. Geraint Williams (London, 1993), pp. 197–227.

14 George Campbell, *Memories of My Indian Career* (London, 1893), I, p. 59.

15 Lata Man, 'Contentious Traditions: The Debate on Sati in Colonial India,' in *Recasting Women: Essays on Indian Colonial History*, ed. Kumkum Sangari and Sudesh Vaid (New Brunswick, 1990), pp. 88–126.

16 Quoted in Richard Koebner and Helmut Dan Schmidt, *Imperialism: The Story and Significance of a Political Word, 1840–1960* (Cambridge, 1964), pp. 136–7.

17 J. R. Seeley, *The Expansion of England* (London, 1925), p. 350.

18 See Koebner and Schmidt, *Imperialism*, pp. 173–5.

19 Quoted by Thomas R. Metcalf, *Ideologies of the Raj*, Vol. II. 4 of *The New Cambridge History of India* (Cambridge, 1994), p. 34.

11. ENDING

1 See Efraim Karsh and Inari Karsh, *Empires of the Sand: The Struggle for Mastery in the Middle East 1789–1923* (Cambridge, Mass., and London, 1999).

2 Jonathan D. Spence, *The Chan's Great Continent: China in Western Eyes* (New York and London, 1998), p. 101.

3 Quoted ibid., pp. 99–100.

4 Paul Kennedy, *The Rise and Fall of the Great Powers* (New York, 1987), pp. 148–9.

5 *Imagined Communities: Reflections on the Origins and Spread of Nationalism*, rev. edn (London, 1991).

6 Recorded by Peter Fry in 'Spirits of the Hills', *Times Literary Supplement*, 7 April 2000, p. 22.

7 Anthony D. Smith, *National Identity* (London and New York, 1991).

8 Cf. J. C. Lescure, 'Faire les Italiens', in *L'Europe des nationalismes aux nations* (Paris, 1996), II, p. 9. The remark has also been attributed to Carlo Cattaneo and Massimo d'Azeglio.

9 *Correspondence*, ed. G. Roth (Paris, 1955), VIII, p. 16.

10 For the most recent, overstated and hysterical expression of this fear, see Michael Hardt and Antonio Negri, *Empire* (Cambridge, Mass., and London, 2000).

11 *Our Global Neighbourhood: The Report of the Commission on Global Governance*, with an introduction by Nelson Mandela (Oxford, 1995).

12 John Rawls, *The Law of Peoples* (Cambridge, Mass., and London, 1991).

Bibliography

Albert, S., *Bellum Iustum*, Frankfurter Althistorische Studien, 10 (Kallmunz, 1980).

Anderson, Benedict, *Imagined Communities: Reflections on the Origins and Spread of Nationalism*, rev. edn (London, 1991).

Armitage, David, 'The British Conception of Empire in the Eighteenth Century', in *Imperium/Empire/Reich: Ein Konzept politischer Herrschaft im deutsch-britischen Vergleich*, ed. Franz Bosbach and Hermann Hiery (Munich, 1999).

Axtell, James, *The Invasion Within: The Contest of Cultures in Colonial North America* (New York and Oxford, 1985).

Bacon, Francis, *The Works of Francis Bacon*, eds. James Spedding, R. L. Ellis and D. D. Heath, 14 vols (London, 1857–74).

Bailey, Cyril (ed.), *The Legacy of Rome* (Oxford, 1923).

Barker, Ernest, 'The Conception of Empire', in *The Legacy of Rome*, ed. Cyril Bailey (Oxford, 1923).

Bayly, C. A., *Imperial Meridian: The British Empire and the World 1780–1830* (Harlow, 1989).

Blackburn, Robin, *The Making of New World Slavery: From the Baroque to the Modern 1492–1800* (London, 1997).

——, *The Overthrow of Colonial Slavery 1776–1848* (London, 1988).

Boardman, John, *The Greeks Overseas: Their Early Colonies and Trade* (New York and London, 1980).

Boardman, John, Jasper Griffin and Oswyn Murray (eds.), *The Oxford History of the Classical World* (Oxford and New York, 1986).

Bosworth, A. B., *Conquest and Empire: The Reign of Alexander the Great* (Cambridge, 1988).

Botero, Giovanni, *The Reason of State [Della ragion di stato]*, trans. P. J. and D. P. Waley (London, 1956).

Bougainville, Louis-Antoine de, *Voyage autour du monde par la frégate la Boudeuse et la flûte l'Étoile; en 1766, 1767, 1768 and 1769* (Paris, 1980).

Boxer, Charles, *The Dutch Seaborne Empire, 1600–1800* (New York and London, 1970).

Bromwich, David (ed.), *On Empire, Liberty and Reform: Speeches and Letters of Edmund Burke* (New Haven and London, 2000).

Brown, Peter, *Augustine of Hippo: A Biography* (London, 1976).

Burke, Edmund, *Speech of Edmund Burke Esq. on Moving His Resolution for Conciliation with the Colonies* (London, 1775).

——, *The Speeches of the Right Hon. Edmund Burke*, Vol. V 'India, Madras and Bengal, 1774–1785', ed. P. J. Marshall (Oxford, 1981).

——, *The Writings and Speeches of Edmund Burke*, ed. Paul Langford (Oxford, 1981).

Burrow, John, *The Crisis of Reason: European Thought, 1848–1914* (New Haven and London, 2000).

Cambridge History of Africa, general eds. J. D. Fage and Roland Oliver, 8 vols (Cambridge and New York, 1975–86).

Campbell, George, *Memories of My Indian Career*, 2 vols (London, 1893).

Cary, George, *The Medieval Alexander* (Cambridge, 1956).

Condorcet, Marie-Jean, marquis de, *Esquisse d'un tableau historique des progress de l'esprit humain* (Paris, 1793).

Cook, James, *The Journals of Captain James Cook on his Voyages of Discovery*, ed. J. C. Beaglehole, 3 vols (Cambridge, 1955–67).

Corpus Hermeticum, eds. A. J. Festugière and Arthur Darby Knock (Paris, 1954).

Curtin, Philip, *The Image of Africa: British Ideas and Action, 1780–1850* (Madison, 1964).

——, *The African Slave Trade: A Census* (Madison, 1969).

De Brosses, Charles, *Histoire des navigations aux terres australes*, 2 vols (Paris, 1756).

Diamond, Jared, *Guns, Germs, and Steel: The Fate of Human Societies* (New York and London, 1999).

Duverger, Maurice (ed.), *Le concept d'empire* (Paris, 1980).

Edney, Mathew H., *Mapping an Empire: The Geographical Construction of British India 1765–1843* (Chicago and London, 1997).

Elliott, J. H., *Imperial Spain, 1469–1716* (London, 1963).

——, *Spain and its World 1500–1700* (New Haven and London, 1989).

Eltis, David, *Economic Growth and the Ending of the Atlantic Slave Trade* (New York and London, 1987).

Elvin, Mark, *The Pattern of the Chinese Past: A Social and Economic Interpretation* (Stanford, Ca., 1973).

Farge, J. D., *A History of Africa* (London, Melbourne, Auckland, and Johannesburg, 1978).

Fernández Armesto, Felipe, *Columbus* (New York and London, 1991).

Finley, M. I., *Ancient Slavery and Modern Ideology* (New York, 1980).

—— (ed.), *Classical Slavery* (London and Totowa, N.J., 1987).

Fletcher, Andrew, *The Political Works of Andrew Fletcher* (London, 1737).

Fox, Robin Lane, *The Search for Alexander* (Boston, 1980).

Garney, P. A., and C. R. Whittaker (eds.), *Imperialism in the Ancient World* (Cambridge, 1978).

Grant, Michael, *Historical Rome* (Englewood Cliffs, N.J., 1978).

Greenblatt, Stephen, *Marvellous Possessions: The Wonder of the New World* (Oxford, 1991).

—— (ed.), *New World Encounters* (Berkeley, Los Angeles and London, 1993).

Hardt, Michael, and Antonio Negri, *Empire* (Cambridge, Mass., and London, 2000).

Hartogh, François, *Mémoires d'Ulysse: Récits sur la frontière en Grèce ancienne* (Paris, 1996).

Herder, Johann Gottfried von, *Outlines of a Philosophy of the History of Man* [*Ideen zur Philosophie der Geschichte der Menschheit*], trans. T. Churchill (London, 1800).

Hobsbawm, Eric, *The Age of Empire, 1875–1914* (London, 1987).

Kagan, Richard, and Geoffrey Parker (eds.), *Spain, Europe and the Atlantic World: Essays in Honour of John H. Elliott* (Cambridge, 1995).

Kant, Immanuel, *Political Writings*, ed. Hans Reiss (Cambridge, 1991).

Karsh, Efraim, and Inari Karsh, *Empires of the Sand: The Struggle for Mastery in the Middle East 1789–1923* (Cambridge, Mass., and London, 1999).

Kennedy, Paul, *The Rise and Fall of the Great Powers* (New York, 1987).

Khilnani, Sunil, *The Idea of India* (New York, 1997).

Kipling, Rudyard, *A Choice of Kipling's Verse, Selected with an Essay on Rudyard Kipling by T. S. Eliot* (London, 1963).

Koebner, Richard, *Empire* (Cambridge, 1961).

——, and Helmut Dan Schmidt, *Imperialism: The Story and Significance of a Political Word, 1840–1960* (Cambridge, 1964).

Kramer, Paul, 'Making Concessions: Race and Empire Revisited at the Philippine Exposition, St Louis, 1901–1905', *Radical History Review*, 73 (1999).

Las Casas, Bartolomé de, *Historia de las Indias*, ed. Augustín Millares Carlo, 3 vols (Mexico and Buenos Aires, 1951).

——, *A Short Account of the Destruction of the Indies*, trans. Nigel Griffin (London and New York, 1992).

Laurens, Henry, Charles C. Gillispie, Jean-Claude Golvin and Claude Traunecker, *L'Expédition d'Egypte: 1798–1801* (Paris, 1989).

Léry, Jean de, *Histoire d'un voyage faict en la terre du Bresil autrement dite Amerique* (Geneva, 1578).

Lintott, Andrew, *Imperium Romanum: Politics and Administration* (London and New York, 1993).

MacMullen, Ramsay, *Christianizing the Roman Empire A.D. 100–400* (New Haven and London, 1984).

Marshall, P. J., *The Impeachment of Warren Hastings* (Oxford, 1965).

Metcalf, Thomas R., *Ideologies of the Raj*, Vol. II. 4 of *The New Cambridge History of India* (Cambridge, 1994).

Mexia, Pedro de, *Historia imperial y caesarea, en la qual en summa se contiene las vidas y hechos de todos los caesares imperadores de Roma desde Julio Caesar hasta el Emperador Carlos Quinto* (Antwerp, 1561).

Mill, John Stuart, *Utilitarianism, Liberty, Representative Government*, ed. Geraint Williams (London, 1993).

Mommsen, Wolfgang, *Theories of Imperialism*, trans. P. S. Falla (Chicago, 1980).

Nicolet, Claude, *L'inventaire du monde: géographie et politique aux origines de l'empire romain* (Paris, 1988).

Our Global Neighbourhood: The Report of the Commission on Global Governance, with an introduction by Nelson Mandela (Oxford, 1995).

Oxford History of the British Empire, general ed. Roger Louis, 5 vols (Oxford and New York, 1998–9).

Pagden, Anthony, *The Fall of Natural Man: The American Indian and the Origins of Comparative Ethnology* (Cambridge, 1982).

——, 'The "Defence of Civilization" in Eighteenth-Century Social Theory', *History of the Human Sciences*, 1 (1988).

——, *European Encounters with the New World: From Renaissance to Romanticism* (New Haven and London, 1993).

——, *Lords of All the World: Ideologies of Empire in Spain, Britain and France, c. 1500–c. 1800* (New Haven and London, 1995).

Parker, Geoffrey, *Spain in the Netherlands, 1559–1659* (London, 1979).

Poliakov, Leon, *The Aryan Myth: A History of Racist and Nationalist Ideas in Europe*, trans. E. Howard (London, 1974).

Price, Richard, *Political Writings*, ed. D. O. Thomas (Cambridge, 1991).

Raleigh, Sir Walter, *Judicious and Select Essays and Observations* (London, 1667).

Rawls, John, *The Law of Peoples* (Cambridge, Mass., and London, 1991).

Richardson, J. S., '*Imperium Romanum*: Empire and the Language of Power', *Journal of Roman Studies*, LXXXI (1991).

Robertson, John (ed.), *A Union for Empire: Political Thought and the British Union of 1707* (Cambridge, 1995).

Russell, Peter, *Prince Henry 'The Navigator': A Life* (New Haven and London, 2000).

Russell-Wood, A. J. R., *The Portuguese Empire, 1415–1808: A World on the Move* (Baltimore and London, 1992).

Said, Edward, *Orientalism* (New York and London, 1979).

——, *Culture and Imperialism* (New York and London, 1993).

Sangari, Kumkum, and Sudesh Vaid (eds.), *Recasting Women: Essays on Indian Colonial History* (New Brunswick, 1990).

Scammell, G. V., *The World Encompassed* (London and New York, 1981).

Schumpeter, Joseph, *Imperialism and Social Classes*, trans. Heinz Norden (Oxford, 1951).

Seeley, J. R., *The Expansion of England* (London, 1925).

Smith, Adam, *An Inquiry into the Nature and Causes of the Wealth of Nations*, ed. R. H. Campbell and A. S. Skinner, 2 vols (Oxford, 1976).

Smith, Anthony D., *National Identity* (London and New York, 1991).

Smith, Bernard, *European Vision and the South Pacific* (New Haven and London, 1985).

——, *Imagining the Pacific: In the Wake of the Cook Voyages* (New Haven and London, 1992).

Spence, Jonathan D., *The Chan's Great Continent: China in Western Eyes* (New York and London, 1998).

Stein, Burton, *Vijayanagara*, Vol. I. 2. of *The New Cambridge History of India* (Cambridge, 1989).

Subrahmanyam, Sanjay, *The Career and Legend of Vasco da Gama* (Cambridge, 1997).

Tanner, Marie, *The Last Descendant of Aeneas: The Habsburgs and the Mythic Image of the Emperor* (New Haven and London, 1993).

Thomas, Hugh, *The Slave Trade: The Story of the Atlantic Slave Trade: 1440–1870* (New York, 1997).

Tinker, Hugh, *A New System of Slavery: The Export of Indian Labour Overseas 1830–1920* (London, 1974).

Trudel, Marcel, *The Beginnings of New France, 1524–1663*, trans. Patricia Claxton (Toronto, 1973).

Vitoria, Francisco de, *Political Writings*, ed. Anthony Pagden and Jeremy Lawrance (Cambridge, 1991).

Walter of Châtillon, *The 'Alexandreis' of Walter of Châtillon: A Twelfth-Century Epic*, trans. David Townsend (Philadelphia, 1996).

White, Richard, *The Middle Ground: Indians, Empires and Republics in the Great Lakes Region 1650–1815* (Cambridge, 1991).

Williams, Robert A., *The American Indian in Western Legal Thought: The Discourses of Conquest* (New York and Oxford, 1990).

Wood, Gordon, *The Creation of the American Republic 1776–1787* (New York and London, 1972).

Zurara, Gomes Eanes de, *Crónica dos feitos na conquista de Guiné*, ed. Torquato de Sousa Soares (Lisbon, 1961).

Key Figures

Alexander III of Macedon (356–323 BC) called 'the Great', Greek monarch, creator of a vast empire which reached from the Adriatic to the Indus, from the Punjab to the Sudan, the subject of a number of mythical tales about his courage and wisdom, and a hero for many later empire-builders, among others Pompey, Trajan and Napoleon.

Apuleius (c. 125–c. 170) writer and orator, best known for the *Golden Ass*, the only surviving complete Latin novel, as well as a miscellany of declamations, narrative descriptions and anecdotes called the *Florida*.

Aristotle (384–322 BC) Greek philosopher, logician, epistemologist, political theorist, aesthetician, biologist, astronomer. Aristotle not only practised these subjects but in a sense he invented most of them. He had been a pupil of Plato and was the tutor to Alexander the Great (*q.v.*).

Augustine of Hippo, Saint (354–430) one of the Fathers of the church who eventually became Bishop of Hippo in North Africa. He was the author of, among many other works, *The City of God*, and exercised a profound influence on the development of Christian theology.

Augustus (63 BC–AD 14) emperor of Rome, the first to assume the title *princeps* (first among men) and virtual creator of the system and ideology, known as the principate, which dominated the empire during the first three centuries of the Christian era.

Bacon, Francis (1561–1626) English philosopher, scientist and statesman, author among a vast body of writings of the highly influential *Great Instauration* and of series of essays in the manner of Michel de Montaigne.

Bentinck, Lord William (1774–1839) governor-general of Bengal (1828–33) and of India (1833–5), a liberal reformer who attempted to govern India according to Hindu laws, opened up judicial post to Indians and abolished sati, the Hindu practice of widow-burning.

Bolívar, Simón (1783–1830) called 'The Liberator', soldier-statesman and liberator of much of South America from the Spanish.

Borges, Jorge Luis (1899–1986) Argentine poet, writer, essayist, librarian.

Bougainville, Count Louis Antoine de (1729–1811) French mathematician and explorer, and the first Frenchman to circumnavigate the globe. Best known for his description of the pleasures to be found on the island of Tahiti and for having brought the first Bougainvillea to Europe, a plant which is named after him.

Burke, Edmund (1729–97) Irish philosopher, pamphleteer, orator and Whig member of parliament. He pleaded the American case during the War of Independence and organized the impeachment trial of Warren Hastings (*q.v.*). His best-known work, *Reflections on the Revolution in France*, was a fierce and excoriating denunciation of the ideology of the French revolution.

Caesar, Julius (100–44 BC) Roman military leader, conqueror of Gaul and Britain and responsible for the beginning of the end of the Roman republic for which he was assassinated by republican patriots.

Charles I, 'Charlemagne' (742–814) king of the Franks. With the exception of Asturias in Spain, southern Italy and the British Isles, he united almost all the Christian lands in Western Europe. Crowned emperor in 800.

Charles V, Holy Roman Emperor (1500–58) united the kingdoms of Spain, the Netherlands, much of Italy, and all of Central and South America. His was, as the Italian poet Ariosto said of it, an empire 'on which the sun never set'. He abdicated in favour of his son Philip II in 1556.

Cicero, Marcus Tullius (106–43 BC) Roman jurist, orator and philosopher. He wrote treatises on law, politics – the best known being *On*

Duties (*De Officiis*) – and rhetoric, and a large number of speeches which he delivered to the Roman senate. Cicero was a staunch republican and was executed in 43 BC.

Claudian (**Claudius Claudianus**, 370–404) Latin poet and panegyrist.

Columbus, Christopher (**Cristoforo Colombo**, 1451–1506) Genoese navigator who in 1492 became the first historically significant European to set foot in the Americas. Columbus made three subsequent voyages to America, in 1493, 1498 and 1506, and occupied most of Hispaniola (now Haiti and the Dominican Republic). Although by the time of his return from his second voyage, during which he sailed into the Gulf of Paria (Venezuela), it was obvious to almost everyone in Europe that he had come across a 'New World', Columbus insisted until his death that the eastern seaboard of America was in fact the western extremity of Asia.

Constant, Benjamin (1767–1830) Franco-Swiss liberal political theorist and novelist. Passionate in his denunciation of the Napoleonic empire, he became a deputy in the French parliament in 1819 after the fall of Napoleon (*q.v.*), and president of the Council of State in 1830. He is best remembered today for *The Spirit of Conquest and Usurpation and their Relation to European Civilization*, *Principles of Politics Applicable to all Representative Governments*, the *Liberty of the Ancients Compared with that of the Moderns*, and the novel *Adolph*.

Constantine the Great (*c.* 280–337) Roman emperor responsible for the creation of Constantinople (now Istanbul) and for making Christianity the official religion of the empire.

Cook, Captain James (1728–79) English navigator. He made three voyages to the Pacific between 1768 and 1779 during which he circumnavigated Australia and charted much of its coastline. His accounts of his journeys earned him an enormous following in Europe and his death on the beach at Hawaii on his final voyage, at the hands of Hawaiians who may or may not have taken him for their god Lono, has been the subject of a prolonged and heated debate ever since.

Cortés, Hernán (1485–1547) Spanish conquistador who between 1519 and 1521 overran the Aztec empire. He also founded the city of Mexico, created the Spanish settlement of New Spain, and led the first major expedition to Honduras.

Cyrus the Great (r. 559–c. 529 BC) Persian emperor, founder of the Achaemenid empire.

Darius I (550–486 BC) called 'the Great', Persian emperor who extended the empire from the Indus Valley to Macedonia. He began the construction of the great palace at Persepolis and may have been responsible for establishing Zoroastrianism as the official religion.

Diderot, Denis (1713–84) French philosopher, essayist, short-story writer, dramatist and editor, with Jean d'Alembert, of the *Encyclopédie*. He contributed extensively to the Abbé Raynal's (q.v.) massive *Philosophical and Political History of the Two Indies*, one of the most violent condemnations of European colonialism in the eighteenth century, and wrote a fictional supplement to Bougainville's (q.v.) account of his experiences on Tahiti which helped create the myth of the 'noble savage' in the eighteenth century.

Gama, Vasco da (1460–1524) Portuguese navigator who in 1497 was the first European to sail around the Cape of Good Hope and thus establish a sea-route between Europe and India.

Gibbon, Edward (1737–94) one of the greatest of the eighteenth-century historians, best known for *The Decline and Fall of the Roman Empire*, first published in 1776.

Gobineau, Joseph-Arthur, self-styled Comte de (1816–82) French diplomat and social theorist. He wrote a number of stories, histories and literary criticism but is best known for his *Essay on the Inequality of the Human Races* of 1853–5 which is regarded as one of the founding documents of modern racism.

Hakluyt, Richard (1552–1616) English historian and geographer, and propagandist for English maritime expansion, best known as the compiler of the *Principal Naviations, Voyages and Discoveries of the English Nation*.

Hastings, Warren (1732–1818) governor-general of India from 1774–85. On his return to Britain, Hastings was impeached at the instigation of

Edmund Burke (*q.v.*) for misconduct. His trial dragged on from 1788 until 1795 when he was acquitted.

Henry, Prince, of Portugal (1394–1460) sometimes called 'the Navigator', Portuguese prince who sponsored the earlier European voyages down the coast of West Africa, played a decisive role in European involvement in the African slave trade, and opened the way for all future European overseas expansion.

Herder, Johann Gottfried von (1744–1803) German philosopher, historian, theologian, linguist and poet, former pupil of Kant (*q.v.*) and often claimed to be the intellectual founder of modern German nationalism. Best known for *Reflections on the Philosoply of the History of Mankind*, and *Yet Another Philosophy of History*.

Herodotus of Halicarnassus (*c.* 484–420 BC) Greek historian and author of the earliest historical narrative we possess, which is largely concerned with the wars between the Greeks and the Persians.

Hume, David (1711–76) Scottish or 'North Briton' sceptical philosopher, essayist and historian, author of *A Treatise of Human Nature*, *An Enquiry Concerning Human Understanding*, and the multi-volume *History of England*.

Jones, Sir William (1746–94) British orientalist and judge. He was the first man to suggest an association between Greek and Sanskrit, and the existence of an Indo-European family of languages. His *Institutes of Hindu Laws* (1794) greatly influenced British attempts to make the British and Hindu legal systems compatible.

Kant, Immanuel (1632–1704) German philosopher, author of the *Critique of Pure Reason*, the *Critique of Practical Reason* and the *Critique of Judgement* (among many other works) which were responsible for the creation of a system of ethics which still dominates Western liberal ways of thinking.

Las Casas, Bartolomé de (1474?–1566) Spanish Dominican, Bishop of Chiapas in Mexico and 'Apostle to the Indians'. The fiercest and best-known champion of the rights of the American Indians in the sixteenth century, he was a prolific writer and tireless agitator whose efforts had considerable impact on the Spanish administration of the Americas.

Livy (Titus Livius, 59 BC–AD 17) Roman historian, his *Ab urbe condita libri* ('Books from the Foundation of the City') is a celebration of the rise of the empire, in much the same way as is Virgil's (*q.v.*) *Aeneid*.

Locke, John (1632–1704) English philosopher, best known as the author of *An Essay on Human Understanding* and *Two Treatises on Government*. Locke was involved in the settlement of the Carolinas for which he wrote a constitution, and was a shareholder in the Royal Africa Company.

Machiavelli, Niccolò (1469–1527) Florentine political theorist, playwright, diplomat and author, most famously, of *The Prince* and the *Discourses on Livy*.

Magellan, Fernando (Fernão de Magalhães, 1480–1521) Portuguese navigator, left Spain in 1519, discovered the Straits of Magellan and crossed the Pacific. He was killed in the Philippines, but one ship of his fleet returned to Spain in 1522 having completed the circumnavigation of the world.

Maine, Sir Henry (1822–88) English jurist, member of the Law Council of the governor-general of India, responsible for codifying Indian law, first professor of comparative jurisprudence at the University of Oxford, and author of the influential *Ancient Law*.

Malinowski, Bronislaw (1884–1942) Polish anthropologist who spent much of his professional life in London. He was a prolific writer who is generally identified as one of the founders of the 'functionalist' school of British social anthropology.

Mill, John Stuart (1806–73) English utilitarian philosopher, liberal and political economist. Best known for his *Principles of Political Economy* and the essay *On Liberty*.

Montesquieu, Charles-Louis de Secondat, baron de (1689–1755) French jurist and philosopher, the author of *The Sprit of the Laws*, an encyclopaedic study of the social habits and legal systems of the world, which is often considered to be the first work of comparative sociology.

Müller, Max (1823–1900) German orientalist and linguist who spent most of his professional life at Oxford University. His main achievement was the fifty-one volumes of the *Sacred Books of the East* (1879–1904). He also did much to develop the idea of an Aryan race from which the peoples of both India and Europe are descended.

Napoleon Bonaparte (1769–1821) French general, First Consul (1799–1804) and Emperor of the French (1804–14/15). Napoleon attempted to impose the principles of the French revolution upon the whole of Europe. He failed but he helped create the Europe of nations which exists to this day. He also transformed France itself, revised the entire legal system (the Napoleonic Code) and reorganized the system of administration and education.

Ovid (43 BC–AD 17/18) Roman poet, author of the *Metamorphoses*.

Philip II (382–336 BC) king of Macedon and father of Alexander the Great (*q.v.*). He created the formidable Macedonian army with which in August 338 at Chaeronea he won a crushing victory over an alliance of southern Greek cities led by Athens and Thebes. This made Macedon an unchallenged superpower and prepared the way for his son's conquests in Persia.

Philip II (1527–98) king of Spain from 1556 and from 1580 king of Portugal. During his reign the Spanish-Portuguese empire, known collectively as the Catholic Monarchy, achieved its greatest power and extent.

Pizarro, Francisco (*c.* 1475–1541) Spanish conquistador who between 1530 and 1533 destroyed the empire of the Incas.

Plutarch (*c.* 46–120) Roman philosopher, essayist and historian, author of an admiring yet perceptive *Life of Alexander*, best known for his exemplary biographical sketches, the *Parallel Lives*, and a series of ethical reflections, the *Moralia*.

Polybius (*c.* 200–*c.* 118 BC) Greek historian of Rome's rise to Mediterranean dominion.

Raleigh, Sir Walter (1554?–1618) English seaman, adventurer and writer. In 1585 and 1589 he attempted to found a colony on Roanoke Island, which he named Virginia, and in 1595 led an expedition to Guiana in search of the legendary El Dorado (described in fanciful terms in *The*

Discoverie of Guiana of 1596). He returned again in 1616, promising King James I a new Peru. He failed and in 1618 was executed.

Raynal, Guillaume-Thomas, Abbé (1713–96) French historian, social theorist, journalist and pamphleteer. He is best known as the author of the *Philosophical and Political History of the Two Indies*, first published in 1772, a history and fierce critique of European colonization. A later and much enlarged version published in 1780 contained long passages by Denis Diderot (*q.v.*) and others. It was immensely popular, went through thirty editions between 1772 and 1789 and was translated into every major European language.

Scipio Africanus Major, Publius Cornelius (236–184 BC) noted Roman general who defeated the Carthaginian leader Hannibal at the battle of Zama (probably modern Jama) in 202 and occupied part of North Africa, for which he received the sobriquet 'Africanus'. He also led a Roman army against the Seleucid emperor Antiochus the Great in what is now Syria.

Seneca, Lucius Annaeus (*c.* 4/5 BC–AD 65) tragedian, philosopher and tutor to the emperor Nero. He was one of the most important of the Roman Stoics.

Smith, Adam (*c.* 1723–90) Scottish philosopher and political economist, best known for *The Wealth of Nations*, which still exercises a considerable influence over economic thinking, and *The Theory of Moral Sentiments*.

Soto, Domingo de (1494–1560) Spanish theologian, pupil and successor to Francisco de Vitoria (*q.v.*). His *On Justice and Right* became a standard work in sixteenth- and seventeenth-century European universities. Like Vitoria, he questioned the Spanish crown's claim to be the legitimate ruler of the Americas.

Thucydides (*c.* 460–400 BC), with Herodotus (*q.v.*), the greatest of the Greek historians and author of a history of the Peloponnesian war between Athens and Sparta between 431 and 404 BC.

Tocqueville, Alexis de (1805–59) French liberal political philosopher and statesman, best known as the author of *Democracy in America* and the *Old Regime and the Revolution*.

Trajan (Marcus Ulpius Trajanus, 53–117) Roman emperor during whose rule the empire reached its greatest extent.

Vieira, Antonio (1608–97) Jesuit missionary, orator and diplomat, often thought to be the originator of the Brazilian national mystique of the single nation of mixed bloods, European, African and Amerindian.

Virey, Jules-Joseph noted French physician, author of two works, the *Natural History of the Human Species* (1824) and 'On the Causes of Sociability in Animals and Civilization in Men' (1841), which claimed that there existed marked physiological differences between different races which determined their aptitude for 'civilization'.

Virgil (70–19 BC) Roman poet, best known for his epic on the founding of Rome, the *Aeneid*.

Vitoria, Francisco de (c. 1485–1546) Spanish theologian, author of a number of writings questioning the legitimacy of the Spanish conquest of America which had a lasting influence on the subsequent creation of international law.

Xerxes I (Khshaiarsha, c. 519–465 BC) son of Darius I (q.v.), king of Persia from 486 BC. In 480 he led a massive army into Greece, laid waste to most of Attica and burned the Acropolis in Athens; but his fleet was destroyed at Salamis in September 480 in a battle which decided the future of the Greek world.

Chronology

513 BC	Darius I, Persian emperor, crosses the Bosphorus into Europe
480 BC	Battle of Salamis; Greeks destroy the Persian fleet, thus averting a full-scale invasion
334 BC	Alexander the Great crosses the Dardenelles and begins the destruction of the Persian empire
323 BC	death of Alexander the Great
168 BC	Battle of Pydna; Roman armies put an end to the Macedonian monarchy
44 BC	assassination of Julius Caesar
27 BC	creation of the Roman principate under Octavian
AD 212	the Roman emperor Caracalla extends citizenship to all free inhabitants of the empire
324	Constantine the Great founds a new capital at Byzantium and names it Constantinople
410	Alaric the Goth sacks Rome; Roman rule comes to an end in the West
528	Justinian, emperor in the East, begins the codification of all Roman law
800	Charles I ('Charlemagne'), king of the Franks, crowned by the pope as emperor
1071	Seljuk Turks take Jerusalem
1095–1291	eight major crusades, armed expeditions under the aegis of the papacy, attempt unsuccessfully to recover Jerusalem
1405–33	voyages of the treasure fleet of the admiral Zheng He
1453	Ottoman Turks seize Constantinople, rename it Istanbul and put an end to the Byzantine empire

1492	Christopher Columbus' first transatlantic voyage
1498-9	Vasco da Gama sails to India via the Cape of Good Hope
1519	Charles of Habsburg elected Holy Roman emperor
1519-22	Spanish fleet under Fernão de Magalhães (Magellan) completes first circumnavigation of the globe
1521	Spanish forces under Hernán Cortés overthrow the Aztec empire; Martin Luther appears before the Diet of Worms
1529	Ottoman army of Suleiman the Magnificent lays siege to Vienna
1533	Francisco Pizarro seizes the Inca capital of Cuzco
1534	first voyage of Jacques Cartier to the Gulf of St Lawrence
1580	Philip II of Spain conquers Portugal thus uniting the empires of the two kingdoms
1581	Dutch declare independence from Spain
1583	Sir Walter Raleigh's expedition to Guiana
1600	charter of the East India Company
1607	English settlement at Jamestown
1618	outbreak of the Thirty Years War
1620	voyage of the *Mayflower*
1648	conclusion of the Thirty Years War, Treaty of Westphalia, creation of the system of European states
1668	East India Company takes over Bombay
1690	English settlement at Calcutta
1756	outbreak of Seven Years War
1760	New France surrenders to the British
1763	Peace of Paris brings Seven Years War to an end, leaving Britain in possession of most of North America
1768	Captain Cook's first voyage
1771	publication of Antoine de Bougainville's *Voyage autour du monde*
1772	Cook's second voyage
1776	Declaration of American Independence; publication of Adam Smith's *The Wealth of Nations*, Edward Gibbon's *Decline and Fall of the Roman Empire*; start of Cook's last voyage
1779	death of Cook in Hawaii

1788–95	trial of Warren Hastings, governor of Bengal
1789	beginning of the French revolution
1791	slave revolt in Santo Domingo
1793	Lord Macartney's embassy to China
1803	beginning of the Napoleonic Wars
1806	Holy Roman empire comes to an end
1807	abolition of the slave trade in the British Empire
1810–21	Spanish-American Wars of Independence
1815	Battle of Waterloo, end of Napoleonic Wars, Napoleon exiled to the island of St Helena; Britain takes control of the Cape Colony (South Africa) from the Dutch
1829	sati abolished
1830	French occupy Algeria
1839–42	Opium War between Britain and China
1853	David Livingstone crosses the continent of Africa
1858	abolition of the East India Company
1859	publication of Charles Darwin's *On the Origin of Species*
1869	opening of the Suez Canal
1876	Queen Victoria becomes empress of India
1888	abolition of slavery in Brazil
1890	Cecil Rhodes made prime minister of Cape Colony
1900	Boxer 'rebellion' in China
1908	end of the Ottoman sultanate and creation of the modern Turkish republic
1911	abolition of the Chinese monarchy
1914–18	First World War
1917	creation of the USSR
1939–45	Second World War
1944	Bretton Woods Conference establishes World Bank and International Monetary Fund
1945	establishment of the United Nations
1947	partition and independence of India and Pakistan
1948	independence of Ceylon, renamed Sri Lanka in 1972
1949	establishment of the People's Republic of China
1957–66	independence of the Sudan, the Gold Coast (Ghana), Malaya, Nigeria, Cyprus, Jamaica, Trinidad, Kenya,

	Zanzibar, Algeria, the Congo, Tanganyika, Gambia, Lesotho, Bechuanaland, Botswana, Guiana, Barbados, Mauritius, Northern Rhodesia (Zambia)
1989	fall of the Berlin Wall
1991	dissolution of the USSR
1994	Nelson Mandela becomes president of South Africa, thus ending the rule of the last settler population in Africa
1997	end of British rule in Hong Kong
1999	end of Portuguese rule in Macao

Index